Accounting Ethics

Jack Maurice

*Head of Professional Ethics, The Institute of Chartered Accountants
in England and Wales, and
Secretary, Chartered Accountants Joint Ethics Committee*

PITMAN
PUBLISHING

London · Hong Kong · Johannesburg · Melbourne · Singapore · Washington DC

PITMAN PUBLISHING
128 Long Acre, London WC2E 9AN
Tel: +44 (0)171 447 2000
Fax: + 4 (0)171 240 5771

A Division of Pearson Professional Limited

First published in Great Britain in 1996

ISBN 0 273 62224 2

British Library Cataloguing in Publication Data
A CIP catalogue record for this book can be obtained from the British Library

10 9 8 7 6 5 4 3 2 1

Typeset by Avocet Typeset, Brill, Aylesbury, Bucks
Printed and bound in Great Britain by Bell and Bain Ltd, Glasgow

The Publishers' policy is to use paper manufactured from sustainable forests.

CONTENTS

FOREWORD

BY BRIAN CURRIE

Deputy President, The Institute of Chartered Accountants in England and Wales

This is a book about the ethics of the accountancy profession. The UK accountancy profession is around 200,000 strong. All its members regard their ethical values as the binding force which unites them and separates them from the non-qualified.

The profession has always taken the ethical high ground. This has a number of consequences. Its members in every walk of life have a considerable influence on the commerce and institutions of the communities in which they live and work. It is a vast influence for good. How often businesses and managers in every walk of life turn away from dubious courses because their accountant, whether colleague, adviser, employee or professional auditor, advises them to do so. The size and impact of this force for good can never be measured.

At the same time, because the profession has taken the high ground, it is often challenged by critics. It needs rules of conduct which are effective and are seen to be effective.

There are two great tests of an effective set of rules. First, are the rules accepted and judged appropriate and reasonable both by the public and by those who have the duty to comply with them? Second, if they are breached, is it reasonably simple to determine whether they have been breached (detection) and to prove it in the forum where sanctions are to be applied (prosecution and judgment)? That is the constant challenge facing those who make the profession's ethical rules.

The ethical codes of the accounting profession have greatly changed in the last few years. The underlying principles have remained constant. But the application of the principles and their consequences have changed and are still changing. Challenges from within the profession, from the world at large, from the media and from politicians have increased and will continue to do so. Much progress has been achieved. Much is yet to do.

In the light of all the changes, it is rather surprising that the last book on professional ethics for the accounting profession was published as long ago as 1969. Since 1969 change has been accelerating. The old rules about competition and advertising have faded, particularly in the face of modern competition law. New and clearer thinking has developed in vital areas concerning objectivity and independence. New areas of practice have become mainstream, raising fresh ethical issues. An enormous proportion of the profession's members are now outside the old practice areas, yet regard their ethical standing as a foundation for the way they run their affairs.

Jack Maurice has aimed in this book to provide a summary that is up to date, detailed and comprehensive while remaining readable and down-to-earth. He has aimed not only at the profession – professional accountants and students – but at all those who work with accountants. I believe his book will help members of other professions, users of services, employers and others to learn more about the ethos and culture shared by the six UK and Irish professional bodies who form the Consultative Committee of Accountancy Bodies (CCAB).

I enjoyed working with Jack Maurice while I was a member of the Chartered Accountants' Joint Ethics Committee (CAJEC). As the Committee's Secretary he, and his assistants, represented a fund of experience and knowledge which was crucial to us in our task. This is because, in addition to serving the committees that form the rules, they man the telephone lines and enquiry desks that deal with the ethical questions and problems posed by practitioners, non-practitioners and the public. This gives them an understanding for the issues and pressures of the market-place far beyond that of any single member alone.

This richness of understanding comes through in Jack Maurice's book, particularly in the brief case studies and analyses which he has added to so many of his chapters.

In addition to his long and deep experience of our profession, Jack Maurice is a barrister by background. This has always sharpened his eye for our institutions and sometimes his tongue. Some of his judgements are mordant. Some are trenchant. This makes him entertaining to read and stimulating to work with. We have never agreed about everything and some passages in his book are no exception. But I admire the robust way he raises the questions and backs his viewpoint.

This book should set us all thinking. We can ask for nothing better than that.

ACKNOWLEDGEMENTS

My special thanks to:

Liz Le Breton, my literary agent, without whose commitment *Accounting Ethics* would certainly not have achieved publication;

Brian Currie, for agreeing to contribute the Foreword, and to both him and Caroline Russell for having the patience to read through the text and make considered and helpful comments;

Patrick Bond and Lisa Howard of Pitman Publishing, for their enthusiastic collaboration;

Gill Seago, for perseverance in the word-processing;

ICAEW, for their permission to reproduce the *Guide to Professional Ethics*;

and finally – but by no means least – to my long-suffering wife, family, colleagues, and my old and trusted friends, for their unfailing encouragement.

CHAPTER 1

The ethics of a profession

To understand the ethics of the accountancy profession in the United Kingdom – or, for that matter, anywhere else in the developed nations of the world – a general acquaintance with the profession itself, and in particular the practising element in the profession, is more important than an appreciation of ethical theory. Accordingly this book will commence with an overview of the UK profession, which will be followed, in the two succeeding chapters, by consideration of the relevant ethical concepts.

A second contention, or warning is that an understanding of the ethics of any established profession, even of the 'commercial' professions of law and accountancy, is unlikely to be achieved by an approach based on a study of 'business ethics'. The ethical requirements or rules of these professions are specific rather than speculative, finite rather than open-ended, and they are enforced by the professional bodies upon their members, rather than left to the conscience of the marketplace or – in those limited areas where 'business ethics' are underwritten by legal requirements – the courts.

However, since the majority of members of the UK accountancy profession are in fact not engaged or employed in professional practice, but in business or in the public sector, the fact that these non-practising members are themselves subject to professional guidance and discipline does have implications for the wider business community. Professional accountants who are involved in the management of companies are subject to a duty to do their best to ensure that the corporate culture of their organisation does not conflict with the ethical requirements to which they are personally subject, and if they are not successful in that endeavour they are bound to distance themselves from what their professional bodies regard as impropriety, if necessary by withdrawing from that involvement. So the existence of these individual professional centres of excellence within the broader corporate governance of UK organisations *should* contribute, progressively, to a rise in those ethical standards which may be shared between professional and non-professional. Since, as we shall see in Chapter 2, some elements of professional ethics are derived from law, there should also be a greater enthusiasm among those involved in corporate governance for the identification of and compliance with legal requirements, irrespective of the likelihood of discovery and prosecution of any breaches. 'Professional' directors have to be more cognisant of the legal requirements affecting their companies because of their professional training and, indeed, in many respects failure on their parts will be punished by the courts more severely than that of their fellow directors who are not accountants or lawyers. And finally, a conviction of a criminal offence by an accountant or lawyer is likely to have adverse professional repercussions.

THE DEVELOPMENT OF THE UK ACCOUNTANCY PROFESSION

There will be several references to the 'Anglo-Saxon profession' in the course of this book. That term should be construed widely rather than literally. In addition to the United Kingdom, Ireland and the United States, the Anglo-Saxon accountancy profession can conveniently be taken to include the professions of most of those countries over which the Union Jack has flown! In addition to the obvious nations such as Australia and Canada, one should also include New Zealand, South Africa and Zimbabwe – with whom one or other of the UK bodies have reciprocity of membership – Hong Kong, Israel, much of the Caribbean, and, arguably, some of Latin America! The counterweight to the Anglo-Saxon profession is the 'Continental profession', spearheaded by France, Italy and Portugal, where auditors are traditionally and/or by legislation discouraged from providing any additional services to audit clients.

In a little over a century, the Anglo-Saxon accountancy profession has developed from small groups of practitioners in Scotland, Ireland and England applying for and being granted the status of a royal charter to carry out their work (in England the first concern was, surprisingly, insolvency work), to encompass vast multinational financial conglomerates, with household names like Arthur Andersen, Coopers & Lybrand, Ernst & Young, Peats, Price Waterhouse and Touche Ross. These 'Big Six' firms have fee income measured in billions of dollars, employ hundreds of thousands, and have a presence in the majority of the world's principal cities. Their activity is mirrored by tiers of essentially regional or national-based accountancy firms (many of them members of international marketing groups or 'associations'), scaling down, ultimately, to two- or three-partner firms and sole practitioners, some of whom will specialise in, for example, the accounts of doctors and dentists, and others who will be doing their best to maintain traditional general practices against an increasing host of regulatory requirements. In the United Kingdom there are, still, somewhere between ten and twenty thousand such sole practitioners, depending on your basis of assessment and, in particular, whether you are including part-time practitioners who may be completing half a dozen sets of tax returns as a sideline to their main employment. The ethical guidance of the professional accountancy bodies does not, in general, differentiate between these marginal practitioners and Andersens. However, the rise of delegated 'self-regulation' has made life much more complicated for those practitioners, full or part-time, who continue to practise in what have become *reserved areas* (see Chapter 3).

One of the most important characteristics of the 'Anglo-Saxon' accountancy profession is that it believes that it is in the interests of both clients and the public that accountancy firms should be able to provide a range of accountancy services, and that most of that range should be available to *audit* clients if they should wish it. Some understanding of the work of the auditor, and the special significance attached to it by the accountancy profession, is necessary to any understanding of the profession's ethical regime. However, before we come to focus on accountancy services – and audit in particular – it will be helpful to take a bird's-eye view of the organisation of the accountancy profession in the United Kingdom, and the recognised professional bodies who control it.

THE CONSULTATIVE COMMITTEE OF ACCOUNTANCY BODIES (CCAB)

The six professional bodies which make up the Consultative Committee are:

The Institute of Chartered Accountants in England and Wales (ICAEW)
The Institute of Chartered Accountants of Scotland (ICAS)
The Institute of Chartered Accountants in Ireland (ICAI)
The Chartered Association of Certified Accountants (ACCA)
The Chartered Institute of Management Accountants (CIMA)
The Chartered Institute of Public Finance and Accountancy (CIPFA)

The greatest community of interest is between the four auditing bodies: ICAEW, ICAI, ICAS and ACCA. The particular areas of activity of CIMA and CIPFA members are explicit in their titles. It is worth noting at this stage that the core ethical guidance of ICAEW, ICAI and ICAS is effectively identical, and that the three bodies seek to harmonise all their ethical requirements via the Chartered Accountants Joint Ethics Committee (CAJEC). The ethical requirements of ACCA are similar in most respects to those of 'the three'. (Significant differences between CAJEC and ACCA requirements will be **highlighted** in the course of the book.)

CCAB came into existence in the early 1970s, following unsuccessful attempts by the profession to achieve fusion. Government pressure was a significant element in the creation of CCAB, and the understandable desire of the Department of Trade to be able to deal with one accountancy organism rather than six has, no doubt, contributed to its continuance. Most technical standard-setting activities are carried out via CCAB, and there has been some (variable) degree of liaison on ethical issues, currently through what is called the CCAB Ethics Liaison Committee. Representation of the UK accountancy profession in Europe (through FEE, the Fédération des Experts Comptables et Economiques Européens) and internationally (as members of IFAC – the International Federation of Accountants) is effected through CCAB.

From time to time efforts have been made to strengthen the CCAB link or umbrella, either for particular projects – the first comprehensive ethical Statement on Professional Independence was achieved via a CCAB working party as recently as October 1979 – or for organisational fusion. In 1993/94 the Bishop working party sought to produce a merger plan for all six bodies. The Bishop proposals have not enjoyed general acceptance among the CCAB six, but have led to other proposals for restructuring which are still underway. At various times ICAEW has sought a closer relationship with each of the other bodies, the possibility of a CIMA/ICAEW merger being recently pursued.

The costs associated with self-regulation are powerful arguments for closer co-operation, particularly between the four auditing bodies. However, traditional sensibilities about the descriptions 'Chartered' and 'Certified' have tended to get in the way. In practical terms, as we shall see, the ethical and technical requirements affecting members of the 'four' are very similar. That is as well, since there are more than 1,000 'mixed' firms of, for example, chartereds plus certifieds, ICAS plus ICAEW, for whom life could be quite difficult if the requirements were conflicting!

A PROFESSION OF AUDITORS?

The development of the UK accountancy profession has, in many ways, paralleled the development of that Anglo-Saxon creation, the joint-stock company. Just as the United Kingdom population has an incidence of registered companies many times greater than any other country of comparable size, so the UK accountancy profession is stronger in numerical terms, at around three professional accountants per one thousand of population, than anywhere else in the world – with the exception of New Zealand and Australia! (The reasons for the pre-eminence of New Zealand in this connection are a topic of some potential interest. Is it related to what might be called the 'Scots factor'?) One much publicised statistic was that, at the height of the accountancy boom of the 1980s, one UK firm (KPMG Peat Marwick) recruited more than 1,000 graduates in one year.

However, as we have noted, less than half of the UK population of professional accountants are engaged in or employed in practice. The rest are in all manner of commercial activities, from proprietor-run art galleries to the boards of all major PLCs. Their activities encompass academic research, government and local authority service, financial controllerships/directorships, forensic accounting, all manner of business enterprises and 'consultancy' activities. It is in connection with the last-mentioned category that real problems of demarcation arise. The professional bodies are not, in general, so much concerned with the status of their members in the financial and commercial world, as whether or not they are *engaging in practice*. This is not just true of the three out of four auditing bodies who have a practising certificate 'regime', but applies also to the fourth, ICAI (the only one of the four to carry out comprehensive practice review) and to CIMA, who impose additional ethical requirements on the small, but rising proportion of their members deemed to be 'in practice'. Accordingly all those bodies have been troubled, from time to time, by the difficulty of defining 'practice'.

The problem is not just academic. The bodies impose requirements for professional indemnity insurance on all members carrying out practice activities. Further, eligibility for a practising certificate, in those bodies that issue them, includes a requirement for completion of post-qualification training which many members, who proceeded straight from qualification to promising positions in industry, do not currently possess and, under the prevailing requirements, will not be able easily to achieve.

The usual elements in a definition of engaging in accountancy practice are:

1 the provision as a principal of;
2 accountancy services (as defined);
3 personally and directly to the public; and
4 otherwise than as an employee.

The principal difficulty is, of course, the definition of 'accountancy services' (2). Here the (otherwise commendable) proliferation of 'consultancy' activities by members creates all sorts of problems. Is it sufficient to require that, to constitute the provision of accountancy services, the relevant consultancy activity should 'be primarily accountancy-based'? Probably not – because there are many activities to which someone trained as a professional accountant would naturally apply accountancy skills: for example, advice on taxation aspects, or corporate strategy, which, say, a lawyer and a marketing specialist respectively would approach from a 'non-accountancy' aspect. And how about IT applications? These days, computer literacy is an essential element in the training of professional accountants, but would advice on suitable hardware and systems, installation, and training of a client's workforce amount to an 'accountancy activity'? Again, the ranks of merchant banking and other finance houses are peppered with professional accountants.

So, does any definition of engaging in public practice require there to be specific exemptions for such activities as the provision of general IT support, finance or insurance? And if you seek to exempt finance and insurance, can you reconcile such an exemption with the status of ICAEW, ICAS, ICAI, and ACCA as recognised professional bodies who authorise their member firms to provide investment business advice under the Financial Services Act 1986, including advice on insurance investments, where that is 'ancillary to accountancy practice'?

ICAEW currently addresses the problem by means of a 'Council Statement' which indicates the parameters but does not purport to be all-embracing. And – in the context of (discontinued) concessions allowing members to provide a few hundred pounds worth of advice annually without a practising certificate – the Statement does include specific exemption for what has been called 'the village audit': that is, work for small communal, charitable, religious and sporting organisations outside the reserved areas, provided free or for a nominal amount.

Let us now return to what is on any account a core accountancy activity, *audit*. In the 1880 Royal Charter of the ICAEW, the functions of 'the Profession of Public Accountants in England and Wales', which 'are of great and increasing importance' emphasise the roles of liquidators, receivers and trustees in bankruptcy, together with 'arrangements with creditors and … various positions of trust under Courts of Justice'. It is almost as an afterthought that reference is made 'also' to 'the auditing of the accounts of public companies and of partnerships and otherwise'. The late Victorian boom in commercial activity, and the geometrical rise in the numbers of UK-registered companies, increased the emphasis on the activities of professional accountants as auditors, while successive Companies Acts underwrote the monopoly in auditing enjoyed by the three Institutes, which were joined in due course by the Association.

There is a *public-interest* element in the carrying on of all the acknowledged professions. This is more apparent in the case of auditing than for any other professional activity, in that the auditor's report is provided not just for the client company, but is also available to potential creditors and investors in the company, and is an essential adjunct to regulation of corporations. It is also *continuing*. These two elements have contributed to a particular status and significance for the auditing activities of professional accountants that exist irrespective of what the law may say at any particular time about the nature and extent of an auditor's duty of care. We shall be investigating the special status of audit work from the point of view of professional independence and objectivity in Chapter 4.

Auditing is still the most significant individual activity of firms of public accountants. However, there will now be very few firms in which auditing occupies more time than all the other activities carried on by the firm. So far as the major firms are concerned, the growth of specialist consultancy activities – sometimes carried on within the main firm, sometimes by 'satellite' practices or companies – has led in recent years to income from audit sinking below 50 per cent of the whole.

Smaller firms, whose consultancy activities are not so extensive and diverse, might be expected to spend more time on audit work. However, recent 'small company' exemptions from audit, which have reduced the number of clients who require an audit as such (although the role of the 'independent reporting accountant' required for companies whose turnover does not exceed £350,000 is still very close to audit), have resulted in many sole and small practitioners having only a dozen or so 'audit clients'. In addition, the comparatively onerous regime of audit registration introduced by the 1989 Companies Act has resulted in many small firms taking a business decision to withdraw from statutory audit work.

The shrinkage in audit may not be of enormous overall significance. Large firms set their standards, compliance and technical, largely by reference to audit work, and carry on a variety of other reporting roles that are treated by the ethical guidance as effectively on the same footing as audit. Smaller firms have traditionally had a greater involvement in the accounting affairs of their (generally smaller) clients, in relation to which the audit report could be regarded as 'the icing on the cake'. But, for all sizes of firms who continue to seek and to accept audit appointments, the role still has what might appear to non-accountants to be a magic and mystery. It is as much on the public record, and as favourable or detrimental to the interests of the parties most concerned, as the decisions of judicial tribunals or the reports of DTI inspectors, and when corporate mega-collapses occur, the first tide of criticism flows, not against the directors as you might expect, but against the auditors.

The ethical guidance of the auditing bodies reflects that public and private accountability, as the next half-dozen chapters will reveal. Architects are said to be sensitive to the fact that their work is always on public display. However, the work of the auditor is also 'on show to the public' and the total financial consequences of getting the figures wrong or drawing the line in the wrong place are quite likely to be even more horrendous than, say, the over-application of high-alumina concrete.

A final consideration which marks out audit as being a special kind of service is that audit firms are currently debarred by statute from limiting their exposure to claims of audit negligence.

Topics for Discussion/Consideration

1 *The auditing profession in the United Kingdom is regulated by (at least) four 'parallel' bodies. Is there any comparable parallel regulation in other professional disciplines?*

2 *There are some professional disciplines, e.g. the Bar, where the practitioner is effectively restricted to the provision of one service. That is the case in relation to the auditing professions in Germany, Italy and Portugal. Does such 'specialisation' add status to the relevant professional role? Does it carry the risk of creating a professional 'ivory tower'?*

3 *Bodies regulated by royal charter, such as the accountancy bodies, are subject to oversight by the Privy Council – but do not have the compensating advantage of a statutory base for their activities. (The situation will be explored further in the next two chapters.) What are the advantages of 'chartered status'? Would the control of auditing be better placed in the hands of a 'General Audit Council'?*

CHAPTER 2

The nature and development of professional ethics

DEFINING ETHICS

The Shorter Oxford Dictionary gives a number of definitions:

The science of morals (1602).

The rules of conduct recognised in certain limited departments of human life (1789).

The science of human duty in its widest extent, including, besides ethics proper, the science of law whether a civil, political or international aspect (1690).

The second definition is the most relevant when one is talking about professional ethics, that is, the rules of conduct recognised in the human life department of the practice of professional accountancy. This is close to the original Greek *ethos*, and one may talk about 'the ethics of a profession' and 'the professional *ethos*' interchangeably. 'Ethos' had the original meaning of 'character', and it is the plural which denotes manners or etiquette. Those definitions of ethics which are close to 'general moral behaviour', or 'right and wrong' are not so helpful in identifying the nature of professional ethics, although they are essential to speculation on what *business ethics* may amount to.

As we shall see at the end of this book, there are developed international ethical guidelines which are mirrored in the codes or guidelines of virtually all the 110 member bodies of the International Federation of Accountants (IFAC). Common threads run through all these national (and international) pronouncements. *Some* of these threads are identifiable as being of absolute moral value – integrity, for example, and objectivity. They are indeed shared by all the recognised professions. However, even such a basic ethical principle as *professional confidentiality* founders, if regarded as an 'absolute', on the Scylla of maintaining client confidence on the one hand, and the Charybdis of the need to disclose information in the public interest on the other!

Ethical theorists point to two different bases for the formulation of ethics: *deontological* – where an ethical requirement is justified because it is a 'good thing in itself'; and *teleological*, where the requirement is neither good nor bad in itself but the intended result is good. (Lawyers identify an equivalent distinction in relation to *evils*, some of which are *evil in essence* (*mala in se*) and others which are prohibited because the *consequences* are evil (*mala prohibitata*).) Requirements based on the need for professional integrity or objectivity would be justifiable on deontological principles. At the other extreme there are requirements generally featured in ethical guidance, such as those relating to practice promotion, where there is no real moral authority for regarding the profession as fundamentally better served by competitiveness on the one hand, or by traditional dignity and restraint on the other, and where accountancy regulators have moved from stringency to licence over three or four years. Pure moral considerations cannot therefore be the sole determinants.

Again, the accountancy profession requires, in the event of change in a professional appointment, a procedure of professional enquiry, by the incoming adviser, in the interests of ensuring that he or she is properly informed as to the circumstances of change. Such a concept would, however, enrage solicitors, who in circumstances of change are instructed to place a premium on continuity of advice to the client. In both of the last-cited instances, there is a practical requirement for the ethical guidance to 'draw a line' (as accountants say). The line must be drawn at a point where it can command the acceptance of a majority of the profession.

ETHICS AND THE LAW

In addition to the contrast with general morality, the requirements of professional ethics are often compared with those of the *law*. The distinction between ethical and statutory requirements is, of course, clearer in the case of the professions whose ethical provisions do not have a statutory basis. Such professions have always required extra restraints from their members beyond those imposed by the law. For example, Companies Act provisions prohibit an officer in a company (or a partner or employee of an officer) from being its auditor. The guidance of the UK accountancy bodies – and indeed that of virtually all other national bodies – warns, in addition, against an auditor being anyone who has a beneficial investment in an audited company, or a substantial mutual business interest with it or with its proprietors. There are, as we shall see, more than a dozen such additional areas of restraint which feature in the UK guidance on audit objectivity and independence, over and above what statute allows or disallows. The bodies justify those restraints in the interest of assisting their members to maintain and, if necessary, demonstrate their objectivity in audit and similar reporting roles. Other restraints may arise from fiduciary roles

– relationships of trust – assumed by accountants towards their clients, for example in advising in the client's best interest, or in relation to accounting to the client for any commission or reward received by the firm arising out of the affairs of the client.

A contrasting, statute-based regime exists in the case of the Conduct Rules of the (English) Law Society, made under the authority of the Solicitors Act. This contains many provisions which are comparable to those in the ethical guidance of the UK accountancy bodies – but the Conduct Rules have, effectively, statutory authority, while the ethical guidance owes its authority to the 'contract' between each member and his or her professional body. When the requirements of professional regulators are similar as well as technical (as is the case in relation to accounting for commission), the distinction between the two regimes may tend to get blurred. The Law Society is, in any event, just as scrupulous in explaining the ethical justification for each set of Rules as are the accountancy bodies in relation to their ethical guidance.

The distinction between 'statute-based' and 'contract-based' regimes is further complicated when it comes to enforcement and discipline. Because breaches of the law committed by members of a profession will tend to bring both them and the profession into disrepute – and this is no less true in the case of professional accountants – a member of one of the UK accountancy bodies who is convicted of a substantial criminal offence faces the sort of double jeopardy which has been previously referred to: he or she will also become the subject of complaint to the Disciplinary Committee of the relevant body. All that really means is that conduct which is illegal is also likely to be, in its essence, unethical. However, the professional tribunal would have scope, even in relation to offences of *strict* liability, to consider a *discretionary* defence: for example, that a member had driven a motor car while uninsured so as to take a critically ill child to hospital to receive urgent medical treatment. That is because the criterion of the professional tribunals is not solely whether an offence has been committed, but whether the profession or member has been brought into disrepute.

THE DEVELOPMENT OF ACCOUNTANCY ETHICS

The professions were, for many years, hidebound by restrictions: on the composition of professional firms (no non-professionals); on practice promotion (no advertising of any kind – letterheadings could not, for example indicate the secretaryship of a local building society); on the names and descriptions under which firms might operate. This was certainly the case for professional accountants in the United Kingdom. Furthermore, access to the professions was traditionally restricted. Sons followed fathers into their practices, and it was important to have the right educational background – the right tie. 'Working-class' accents would contribute to an unacceptable image for many professional practices.

All that changed after the Second World War, when successive Labour (and eventually Conservative) governments preached 'equal opportunities'! The war also produced dramatic advances in technology, and created an atmosphere sympathetic to the development of international trade, so that even in the stuffy old UK business opportunities proliferated. These were accompanied by dramatic growth in the accountancy profession, which enjoyed something like a 250 per cent increase in membership within a generation.

It is very difficult to detect anything like ethical guidance in the UK accountancy profession before approximately 1969 – although there were the restrictions on advertising and promotion already referred to, as well as the requirements for a process of 'professional enquiry on change of appointment'. In particular there was no discernible guidance on professional independence, integrity or objectivity. That is not to say that these elements were not respected. They were, no doubt, taken for granted as part of the professional culture, or 'old boy network'! (Even today, when the relevant guidance Statement runs to 150 clauses, there are senior members who maintain that 'no one who knows me could possibly have any doubt that I shall *instinctively* behave in accordance with the demands of professional independence'!)

A very 'scanty' Guide to Professional Ethics emerged in the ICAEW in that year, and was followed by rather more comprehensive guidance in 1975 when, for the first time, something like the prevailing Statement on Professional Independence was produced. At this point CCAB took an interest, as we have seen, and October 1979 witnessed the approval of a common new Statement entitled 'Professional Independence', which was accompanied by extensive 'explanatory notes'. That guidance was based on the principle that a member should be, *and be seen to be*, free in any professional assignment of any interest which might detract from objectivity. Thereafter, spurred on gently by CCAB, common Statements on confidentiality, practice promotion, names and letterheadings, and specialist forms of practice (mixed, multidisciplinary, management consultancy and data processing) were developed, alongside improved guidance on change in a professional appointment.

Liaison between the secretariats of the CCAB bodies, in particular the auditing 'four', maintained similarity, if not identicality between their ethical guidance through the 1980s – a period which saw great expansion in the range of services provided by accountancy firms (and welcomed by their clients) into such areas as corporate finance, while new legislation, in particular the Financial Services Act and the Insolvency Act (both of 1986), promoted new roles for accountants, together with new ethical guidance necessary to their discharge of those roles.

A very significant further development was the new regime of registered auditors created by the Companies Act 1989, in accordance with the provisions of the European 8th Directive. A wholly revised statement on professional independence – now entitled 'Integrity, Objectivity and Independence' – was required by the Secretary of State as a precondition of recognising the 'four' as qualifying and supervisory bodies under the Act.

The next important development was the creation, by the three UK and Irish Institutes of Chartered Accountants, of the Chartered Accountants Joint Ethics Committee (CAJEC) which has, since its inception in 1990, carried out its own comprehensive review of the rest of the Guide to Professional Ethics shared by the three bodies. This resulted in the removal of a number of obsolete Statements, and additional guidance on conflicts of interest, associations with non-members, and second and other opinions, together with greatly expanded guidance on fees.

Nearly all of the developments referred to above relate to guidance for practising members. However, the 1980s also saw the development of a guidance statement on *ethics for accountants in business*. (Ethics for accountants in business features in Chapter 20.)

With the inception of CAJEC, the pace of development in ethical guidance has increased rather than settled down. Since the Guide to Professional Ethics was reissued in February 1992, the core Statement on Integrity, Objectivity and Independence has seen a host of minor, and several major changes, each of the latter prefaced by extensive consultation within and outside the profession. Substantial additions include a new section on 'Relationships between an audit firm and a company whose officer is a former partner or senior employee', 'Provision of specialist valuations to audit clients', and 'Rotation of audit partners'. All these (as retitled in the latest version of the Statement) will be dealt with in detail in Chapters 5 and 6.

INTERNATIONAL PRESSURES FOR CHANGE

Many of the detailed changes introduced by CAJEC reflect guidance which has already been introduced, or is under consideration elsewhere in the accountancy world. Needs for guidance may be identified by the US AICPA (American Institute of Certified Public Accountants), by the Canadian Institute of Chartered Accountants (CICA) and by the two Australian bodies. None of the world's leading accountancy professions will initiate significant changes in their ethical guidance without consulting with their overseas equivalents. In addition, the Department of Trade keeps aware of transatlantic developments, which may presage changing circumstances and needs in the United Kingdom.

Over the last few years, the International Federation of Accountants (IFAC) has, through its own Ethics Committee, been at pains to monitor developments worldwide, and to incorporate in its own 'model' Code of Ethics all relevant developments in ethical guidance. (These will be dealt with in more detail at the end of the book.)

For all these reasons, the ethics regimes of the accountancy profession, in the United Kingdom and elsewhere, are under continual scrutiny and review, in an attempt to meet changing needs and changing expectations – on the part of clients, the public, the media, and the national and international accountancy regulators. Is all this ethical activity necessary and worthwhile? Perhaps the time has come for a period of calm reflection, and for the hard-pressed practitioner to be given the chance to relax if not vegetate.

The answer is, of course, that this sort of moratorium could not for long withstand those pressures and expectations. And it is not as if the profession itself is unconcerned about ethical issues, and about keeping up-to-date. One manifestation of that is the interest which such developments as *The Framework* have aroused (see Chapter 3). Another is the level of ethical enquiry to the professional bodies. By way of example, the ICAEW, which has two established helplines – CAASE (Chartered Accountants Advisory Service on Ethics) for members in practice, and IMACE (Industrial Members Advisory Committee on Ethics) for members in business – deals with approximately 1,000 ethical enquiries every month. It also distributes more than 14,000 ethical Help Sheets each year on popular areas of enquiry. The Help Sheets are updated at least every six months.

Topics for Discussion/Consideration

1 *Is the pace of change in the UK accountancy profession unique, or is it reflected in changes occurring in, for example, the ethics of the legal profession?*

2 *How far is the current emphasis and concern over accountancy ethics a product of concern about international corporate collapses?*

3 *Does concern at such collapses focus attention on the adequacy or otherwise of the ethical guidance on audit objectivity and independence? Is the current concern about corporate governance, evidenced in the work of the Cadbury Committee, another closely linked factor?*

4 *Does the current high level of international activity in accountancy ethics compared with, for instance, activity in legal ethics, suggest that accountancy has a more international culture and 'language'?*

5 *Would the accountancy profession benefit from having a statutory basis for self-regulation?*

CHAPTER 3

Self-regulation and professional ethics

SELF-REGULATION

Reference has already been made to the increased attention given to the ethical guidance of the accountancy bodies arising from the creation of three statutorily 'reserved' areas in the mid- to late 1980s: investment business advice, insolvency practice, and auditing. In relation to the first area, the bodies have the status of professional bodies *recognised* to authorise firms to carry on investment business ('recognised professional bodies'), and in the second, recognised to license insolvency practitioners. The terminology in relation to the registration of auditors is that of 'qualifying bodies' and 'supervisory bodies'. So far as qualifying bodies are concerned, the four traditional auditing bodies are joined by the Association of International Accountants – a comparatively minuscule body based in Gateshead. (The main purpose of the government's recognition of this 'interloper' may have been to indicate delicately to the CCAB bodies that monopolies should not be regarded as perpetual!) The fifth recognised supervisory body is the Association of Authorised Public Accountants.

This introduction of statute-based roles for the accountancy profession is usually referred to as 'self-regulation', and accordingly, when self-regulation is blamed for changes in the relationship between the bodies and their members, it is the creation of the three reserved areas in the 1980s which is intended. However, in common with all the established professions, the accountancy bodies have undoubtedly been self-regulatory since their inception. Admission to membership, imposition of requirements as to behaviour, and enforcement of those requirements including disciplinary penalties if necessary, are essential elements of all such professions.

As we shall see in Chapter 21, the actual numbers of members who are the subject of adverse findings by the Disciplinary Committees of the bodies have not changed greatly over the years. Nevertheless, the bodies have had to accommodate a plethora of new regulations in their processes, together with arrangements to authorise, license and register, and to monitor those authorised, licensed and registered, in order to ensure that they are fit to remain so.

Probably the main cultural change arising from the 1980s imposition of self-regulation is an extension from governance by *guidance* to governance by *regulations and guidance*. The existing extensive guidance on ethical issues, together with the even more extensive guidance on technical elements, is supplemented, as one might imagine, by Investment Business Regulations, Insolvency Licensing Regulations and Audit Regulations. What was perhaps more unexpected was the proliferation of regulations in other areas:

● Regulations Governing Corporate Practice
● Regulations Governing the Use of the Description 'Chartered Accountant'
● Clients' Money Regulations

(These regulations are not dealt with in detail in this book. Being regulations they must be construed literally and legalistically. ICAEW's CAASE helpline issues useful Help Sheets on each set of regulations.)

If one can identify a common rationale behind the substitution of certain existing guidance provisions by this additional tranche of regulation, it must be that guidance had not proved an adequate basis for enforcement. The advantages and disadvantages of the regulatory approach are illustrated in particular by the last-mentioned – Clients' Money Regulations. They were drafted so as to harmonise as closely as possible with the Investment Business Clients' Money Regulations, deemed a necessary part of the process of investment business authorisation, and indeed deriving their authority from statutory instrument. However, the number of firms holding investment business clients' money is very small – a hundred or so in the case of firms authorised by ICAEW. On the other hand, the number of firms holding *non-investment business* clients' money is very large – virtually all of the six thousand or so firms authorised.

When the inspectors of the Joint Monitoring Unit, set up jointly by ICAEW, ICAI and ICAS, began to visit firms to check on their observance of the requirements relating to investment business, they also, very properly, extended their investigation into the firms' custodianship of *all* their clients' money. This resulted in dozens of references of authorised firms to the Investigation Committee of ICAEW, in most cases for essentially technical breaches of the Clients' Money Regulations not involving any loss of or danger to clients' funds. The increase in complaints of this nature to the Investigation Committee was largely responsible for a decision to introduce 'consent orders', whereby members and firms could agree to be disciplined by the Investigation Committee in comparatively minor cases rather than wait for a 'formal complaint' to be referred to the Disciplinary Committee, and thereby avoid the expense, delay and worry involved in a full disciplinary hearing.

The *advantage* of the regulatory regime in relation to clients' money was that it was very effective in ensuring that defaulters were 'brought to book'. The compensating *disadvantage* was that any real discretion on the part of the Institute in dealing with minor or technical breaches in this area was effectively taken away, and quite large numbers of hitherto blameless members found themselves being criticised, reprimanded and fined by the organisation they had hitherto regarded as their friend and support.

GUIDANCE VERSUS REGULATIONS

Battle is currently being waged in the accountancy profession, and in particular in the United Kingdom, as to the virtues and vices of an approach based on detailed regulations on the one hand, and, on the other, one which depends rather on broader expressions of principle furthered by guidance. The debate probably arose first in relation to ethical requirements on objectivity and independence in particular, but has now certainly spread to technical requirements – especially those relating to auditing, where feelings are running if anything higher.

The ethical climate for the UK accountancy profession has traditionally been largely dictated by *guidance*. As we have seen, however, other professions may be controlled by statute, by regulations – whether arising from statute or otherwise – or by 'rules'. Sometimes the ethical guidance is categorised as a 'Code' (as in the case of the IFAC guidelines) – or a statement or summary of ethical principles labelled 'Code' may be included as part of more comprehensive guidance. Even among the different UK accountancy bodies the terminology varies. ICAEW, ICAI and ICAS share a 'Guide to Professional Ethics'. ACCA is more inclined to refer to 'Rules'. CIMA has 'Guidelines'. They are all, though, in practice talking about much the same thing: authoritative advice or guidance on ethical considerations, failure to follow which renders a member accountable to his or her professional body.

As we shall see in Chapter 21, doing what the Guide (or Rules, etc.) tells you not to do, or failing to do what it requires, would not of itself constitute misconduct, discreditable behaviour, certain liability to disciplinary action, or their equivalents. The effect is that 'in answer to a complaint, a member may be called upon to justify any departure from the guidance' (Introduction to the Guide to Professional Ethics, ICAEW, paragraph 13). That situation has very distinct implications for those in the UK bodies concerned with the disciplinary process: while it will be more difficult – as we shall see – to justify a failure to follow some sections of guidance than others, this possibility of justifying departure from the guidance is always in theory there. Guidance is, at bottom, *advice*.

There are also clear implications for those who seek to draft ethical guidance: they are properly able to seek statements related to the 'principle' and 'spirit' of ethical behaviour, rather than descend to attempting all-embracing, and probably pettifogging, legalisms. They do not have to legislate for every possible situation. Nevertheless, where it is necessary for the guidance to descend to detail, those detailed provisions will still have to be both clear and enforceable if the guidance is to be taken seriously.

The advantages of dealing *in principle*, rather than with a mass of over-whelming *detail*, have been apparent to more than one professional accountancy body for some time. The American Institute of Certified Public Accountants (AICPA) had until recently settled for control by what amounted to *regulations*. As we have seen, for such an approach to be effective the regulatory provisions have to be both comprehensive and closely written. They cannot talk about 'members being guided by the *spirit of the regulations* in any circumstances that are not specifically provided for', as guidance-controlled systems are able to.

Of recent years the AICPA has been aware both of the difficulties of achieving such comprehensiveness, and of the implications of failing to achieve it: situations which slip through the regulations are not in general actionable by the professional body or other regulator against the offender; consulting the ethical requirements comes to mean *finding holes in the regulations*. Any culture of 'seeking the moral high ground' is abandoned in favour of such hole-achieving legalistic approaches, and it has been concluded, on both sides of the Atlantic, that the ethical and moral fibre of the profession is likely to deteriorate as a result. Further, the credibility of the professional regulator is liable to suffer, in the first instance, because as soon as one loophole is exposed and plugged others are discovered, and in the second, because the members of the profession are liable to be perceived as corrupt and opportunist, such a perception being already virtually axiomatic so far as the US legal profession is concerned!

The ensuing moves by the AICPA toward a culture change centred around the preservation by firms of professional objectivity and independence. Though ultimately unsuccessful, they have been a contributor to the emergence of the UK profession's new, principle-based approach to objectivity and independence, the Framework. The new approach is analysed and considered in Chapters 6 and 7.

The time has now come to examine in more detail all the individual elements of the UK ethical regime, and any such examination must commence with – but not restrict itself to – the Guide to Professional Ethics, which has already been mentioned. The Guide, as has been said, is effectively identical for ICAEW, ICAI and ICAS, and the references which follow will be, for convenience, to the ICAEW version. Where the ACCA Rules differ significantly from the Guide, this will be indicated. The Guide consists of an Introduction and

Fundamental Principles, followed by fourteen statements dealing with various detailed ethical aspects.

GUIDE TO PROFESSIONAL ETHICS – INTRODUCTION AND FUNDAMENTAL PRINCIPLES (1.200)

Both of these elements of the Guide have been around for some time, and therefore – assuming that the same longevity parameters apply throughout the Guide – are probably due for review.

The Introduction

The Introduction refers (paragraph 1) to 'the duties owed to the public and to … client or employer' by members, and the requirement 'to observe high standards of conduct which may sometimes be contrary to … personal self interest'.

The Introduction then goes on to indicate the nature and scope of guidance: 'Members should be guided, not merely by the terms, but also by the spirit of this Guide and the fact that particular conduct does not appear among a list of examples does not prevent it from amounting to misconduct.' Having regard to the current debate on 'guidance v. regulations', the Introduction is in fact prescient in pointing out that: 'The value of this approach is that it avoids excessive legalism by not having to anticipate every contingency …' The 'reserved areas of practice' referred to at the beginning of this chapter, which *are* inevitably the subject of a legalistic approach, are also placed in context: 'every effort has been made to harmonise the regulations governing reserved work and the advice contained in this Guide … Should the advice … conflict with the regulation, members are bound to follow the regulation.' Affiliates – see Chapter 21 – are bound by the same provisions as practising members (paragraph 9).

Members in practice overseas

The Introduction then goes on (paragraph 10) to give helpful and practical advice about members practising in overseas jurisdictions. Such members are:

> **required to comply with local laws and should, in a country in which the profession is controlled by a reputable body, adhere to any local ethical guidance or good practice, even though to do so may not be in accordance with the ethical guidance of the Institute.**

This provision is conveniently referred to as the 'when in Rome' provision. It answers the potential criticism that members who regard themselves as subject to the Guide, even though they may be practising in a less restricted environment, could be at a disadvantage compared with local practitioners. In countries where the profession is not so controlled, members should follow the guidance of the Institute 'unless well-established and generally accepted local practice of reputable firms is to the contrary'. However (as we shall see in Chapter 23), this provision is to some extent in conflict with the equivalent provision of the IFAC Code, which requires the standards of the Code, as a universal minimum.

As members of IFAC, the UK professional bodies are committed to applying IFAC standards (as a minimum) in their own jurisdictions. Such incompatibilities – theoretical perhaps rather than practical – should therefore not be allowed to continue. Salvation may be forthcoming from IFAC itself, however, since the IFAC Ethics Committee, at its final meeting, was inclined to favour the UK provision over its own Code requirement.

Failure to follow the guidance

The Introduction has already been quoted in this connection. Failure to follow the Guide means that a member is 'accountable' to the Investigation Committee, but may be able to justify a departure based on the particular circumstances of his or her case (paragraph 13). Paragraph 12 provides that the Disciplinary Committee 'may have regard to any code of practice, ethical or technical and to any regulations affecting member firms laid down or approved by the "Council"'.

This section of the Introduction also contains however what appears to be a further 'wrap-up' provision (paragraph 14):

> **In considering a complaint of misconduct against a member, the Disciplinary Committee may also have regard to the Investment Business, Audit and other Regulations of the Council, the effects of which might otherwise be confined to firms.**

Since 'misconduct' no longer features in the disciplinary provisions of ICAEW, review of terminology is clearly indicated here. Nevertheless the meaning is reasonably clear. On the other hand, there is no mention of codes of practice or regulations which specifically apply to individual *members*. They presumably stand (or fall) as a basis of complaint on their own merits.

Enforcement of ethical standards

The Introduction then summarises the Institute's power to enforce ethical standards, and the functions of the three standing committees: Investigation

Committee, Disciplinary Committee and Appeal Committee. The committees will feature in some detail in Chapter 21. There are references to the 'parallel' procedures of the Joint Disciplinary Scheme, also considered in Chapter 21.

The Introduction ends with a further 'catch-all' provision (paragraph 20), allowing the regulatory committees to take into account failures to follow the Guide, and the injunction (paragraph 21) that: 'A member who is in doubt as to his or her ethical position in any matter may seek the advice of (the) Institute' (by way of the CAASE and IMACE Services – see Chapter 22).

Fundamental Principles

These are five in number, and it is relevant and proper to quote them in full:

1. **A member should behave with integrity in all professional and business relationships. Integrity implies not merely honesty but fair dealing and truthfulness.**
2. **A member should strive for objectivity in all professional and business judgements. Objectivity is the state of mind which has regard to all considerations relevant to the task in hand but no other.**
3. **A member should not accept or perform work which he or she is not competent to undertake unless he obtains such advice and assistance as will enable him competently to carry out the work.**
4. **A member should carry out his or her professional work with due skill, care, diligence and expedition and with proper regard for the technical and professional standards expected of him as a member.**
5. **A member should conduct himself or herself with courtesy and consideration towards all with whom he comes into contact during the course of performing his work.**

(Feminists – or just advocates of fair dealing – may be taken aback by the apparently inconsistent use in the Guide of gender pronouns. The decision to economise with references subsequent to the first is justified as making the guidance 'simpler and more direct'! ICAS has already abandoned this chauvinist technique, and ICAEW will no doubt be forced to follow suit sooner or later.)

Courtesy and consideration

The Fundamental Principles are not just 'declaratory'. In particular, Fundamental Principle 5 ('courtesy and consideration') is frequently used by the Investigation Committee secretariat as a way of bringing persistent non-respondents to book. This is often the case where the failure to respond relates to client correspondence. Where a member fails to respond to Institute correspondence, there is a procedure under paragraph 8(a) of Schedule II to the Bye-Laws (the Investigation/Disciplinary Processes) whereby:

> **The Investigation Committee shall have power to call for, and it shall be the duty of every member and/or firm or student to provide, such information ... as the Investigation Committee may consider necessary to enable it to discharge its functions.**

Competence and regard for technical and professional standards

As is apparent, these essential requirements for any professional (in practice or business) are set out in Fundamental Principles 3 and 4. Failure to follow technical standards is, effectively, actionable by the bodies on the same basis as failure to accord with ethical guidance – the member is 'accountable' to the Institute.

What of a member's failure in these respects so far as his or her exposure to the civil law is concerned? The ethical and technical enquiry services of the professional bodies receive regular queries from solicitors eager to establish such failures to comply – or to discount them, if they are acting for the accountant. The view expressed by the courts has been satisfactorily clear: according with the technical and ethical requirements of the professional bodies is evidence of 'good practice', a failure to accord with them is prima facie evidence of *bad* practice – and the implications as to vulnerability to action for damages follow. It has been pointed out, however, that a member may be able to *justify* a departure from the ethical guidance. (A clear departure from *technical standards* may be more difficult to justify.)

Logically, therefore, a civil claim based on breach of contract or professional negligence evidenced by the *bad* practice of acting in conflict with the Guide should be postponed until possible attempts to justify the departure have been made to a relevant professional body. This creates problems because (as we shall see in Chapter 21) the professional bodies will normally wish to *defer* their own consideration of specific issues which are contemporaneously the subject of civil legal action! Additionally, there is an understandable reluctance for professional accountants to subject themselves voluntarily to the investigative processes of their professional body so as to obtain some sort of 'clearance'. They can, however, seek an authoritative opinion from one of the bodies' professional advisory services (which operate independently of the bodies' investigatory agencies) – although that is wholly dependent on the facts disclosed in the enquiry, which often, alas, prove to be incomplete!

INTEGRITY AND OBJECTIVITY

These elements will be considered at greater length in the next four chapters. It is perhaps worth making a point at this stage about *integrity*. Integrity is not defined in the Guide, even in the Fundamental Principles, or in the subsequent Statement (1.201) 'Integrity, Objectivity and Independence' – save that Fundamental Principle 1 adds that 'Integrity implies not merely honesty but fair dealing and truthfulness'.

Most members of the public would, I believe, *expect* 'integrity' to encompass both 'fair dealing' and 'truthfulness'. Are there any other elements of integrity which one can usefully identify?

Because integrity is rarely assessed and evaluated in Institute tribunals (in the sense that where there has been a clear failure of integrity no one is likely to be in any doubt about it), it may be useful to consider an additional element – namely, of '*professional* integrity', even if it may be more difficult to justify as an element in *basic* integrity. I have been impressed during my years in the Professional Ethics Department of ICAEW by those – both accountants and clients – who have identified *courage*, or at any event 'the courage of one's convictions' as being a highly desirable component, to say the least, of the integrity of an accountant, or indeed of any professional person. It is perhaps therefore appropriate to end this, the last of my introductory chapters, with Polonius's advice, 'to thine own self be true' – even if circumstances and personalities render that course unattractive!

Topics for Discussion/Consideration

1 *What is the balance between regulations and guidance in the governance of other professions?*

2 *Are there disadvantages in the 'when in Rome' provision for practice overseas? Should members of UK accountancy bodies regard the standards of the Guide as a universal minimum?*

3 *Should there be an additional Fundamental Principle or Principles (e.g. confidentiality)?*

4 *How essential is courage on the part of a practitioner, or employed professional, in maintaining (a) the image and (b) the validity of professions?*

Relevant Query

Q. *Is the 'when in Rome' principle applicable to the question of what is, or is not within the definition of 'public practice'?*

A. The definitions of 'public practice' included in the Council Statement in the ICAEW Members' Handbook are not meant to be geographically restricted in their application. However, if, in a country in which the profession is controlled by a reputable body, a specific activity is, as a result of legislation or custom, defined as *not* being a practice activity, then any restrictions associated with practice (such as those on practice promotion and advertising) should not apply.

CHAPTER 4

The special significance of independence and objectivity

PROFESSIONAL INDEPENDENCE AND OBJECTIVITY

Since the inception of the Guide to Professional Ethics, the guidance Statement on professional independence and objectivity has had a position of primacy, both in relation to its location at the beginning of the Guide and its length – it is approximately three times as long as any other Statement. But a bare comparison of the number of pages on independence/objectivity (combined, since 1992 with a repetition of the importance of integrity) with the individual Statements which follow tells by no means the whole truth. The next three Statements in the Guide – on Insolvency Practice, Corporate Finance Advice, and Conflict of Interest – are also concerned essentially with independence/objectivity, though conflict of interest, which is 'lumped in' with independence in most professional disciplines, may have slightly different connotations, at any event for professional accountants.

For many years, until 1992, the Statement on Professional Independence began with the precept that a practising member needed to be *and be seen to be* free from any interest which might detract from his or her objectivity. At the time of formulation of the 1992 guidance, doubts were already being expressed at the practicality and validity of an approach which depended in part on *perceived* independence. After all, whose 'perception' was envisaged? That of the proverbial man on the Clapham omnibus? Or was it that of the more sophisticated City gent in his BMW? Or the City editor of one of the more responsible newspapers?

In addition to the murmurings, on both sides of the Atlantic, about the *validity* of this approach, anxieties were also expressed concerning its *practicality*. The 1980s expansion in accountancy services provided by firms was reflected in a proliferation of possible perceived threats to objectivity, evidenced in the 1992 guidance, not just on its release, but for the following two or three years – with new guidance added on overdue fees, litigation (actual or threatened), influences outside the practice, relationships with a company whose officer was a former partner or senior employee of the firm, and on specialist valuations when provided to audit clients.

There was no reason to believe that there existed a finite list of threats to objectivity, and the Statement was in danger of becoming unmanageable for large firms – and potentially irrelevant to small ones. And consciousness of the principles behind the guidance was receding.

These concerns were reflected in two new 'in principle' approaches. One, by the AICPA, ultimately foundered on the unwillingness of the Securities and Exchange Commission (which oversees listed companies) to countenance the abandonment of detailed provisions and 'prohibitions'. The other is the Framework, which will be investigated in detail over the next three chapters.

What is it about the circumstances applying to professional accountants that has led to this soul-searching about independence and objectivity, and how does the position of the accountant differ from that of members of other professional disciplines in relation to their professions' moves to safeguard objectivity? The most convenient basis for comparison is, once again, that of the legal profession and the preoccupations of the legal regulators on *conflict of interest* situations. That is not to say that the dangers of *getting too near to the client* are totally ignored, for example in the UK Solicitors' Rules. There are warnings against accepting hospitality or loans from a client. It is perhaps significant, however, that the first 'area of risk' identified in the Accountants' Guide to Professional Ethics relates to the proportion of fees from a client or group of clients. In general, lawyers are quite happy to accept any amount of work from existing clients – indeed their sensibilities may be ruffled if a long-established client goes elsewhere for advice in what they consider to be their field. To develop 'client loyalty' solicitors' firms have sometimes maintained unprofitable departments for, say, residential conveyancing, just so that they can provide a totality of service for the directors of their corporate clients. One entire office of a well-known Northern firm of solicitors is given over to the affairs of a local building society. And barristers are, in general, quite happy to depend on particular firms of solicitors for a very significant proportion of their incomes. (An example would be the prosecution-oriented criminal counsel, who receives well over half of his income from the local Crown Prosecution Service.)

It may therefore appear at first sight surprising that this initial situation of risk identified in the Guide specifies 15 per cent as the maximum proportion of fees that an accountant should receive from one audit client or group of clients and, in the case of listed or other public-interest companies, as little as 10 per cent.

THE UNIQUENESS OF THE POSITION OF THE AUDITOR

Mention has already been made of the particular significance that audit holds in the consciousness of the accounting profession. Whereas the work of most professional practitioners centres around, and is largely confined to the interests of the *client*, the accountant must, in audit or similar public-reporting roles, be aware of the public interest in his or her report and the corresponding duty he or she owes to the public. For although the commissioning of the audit report is effectively by the directors, endorsed by the shareholders in General Meeting, the audit report has as much or more significance for two classes of 'outsiders':

1 investors (and potential investors) in the company, including those, such as banks, who provide finance; and
2 those who would do business with the company, or continue to give it trading credit.

The fashionable word that includes these two classes is 'stakeholders', and accountants customarily if not instinctively acknowledge the 'stake' or interest of investors and creditors, whatever the nuances of the law. (That is why the decision in *Caparo* v. *Dickman and others* was greeted with such dismay by certain sections of the profession: they felt that their consciousness of a public duty was in a sense being spurned by the courts.)

Subsequent chapters will deal with the guidance, in particular on 'areas of risk', which constitutes the second part of the Guide's Statement (1.201) on Integrity, Objectivity and Independence. It will, however, be helpful for the reader to return in his or her mind to public interest considerations from time to time, as a sort of touchstone to the aim of the guidance.

'ATTEST' AND 'ASSURANCES'

'Attest' and 'Assurances' are two words used regularly in US accountancy literature in connection with financial reporting activities. The presence or absence of 'assurances' in a professional report has often been expressed as a test of whether or not the report requires 'full independence'. In the Framework, the preservation of *objectivity* has replaced the maintenance of the *appearance of independence* as the principal target of the guidance, for considerations already indicated, while the nuances relating to reporting roles other than audit are dealt with, as in the past, at the beginning of Section B of Statement 1.201.

Audit is often described as the prime 'attest' function. 'Attest' is quite helpful in indicating the status and nature of the audit role, in that it implies acting as a witness or giving evidence. When one seeks parallels with the audit function in other professions, then acting as an *expert witness* is one role that naturally comes to mind: the testimony is on the public record (generally), it is open to 'testing' by an advocate who opposes its conclusions, and it has an associated 'mystery' – the taking of an oath. Clearly the expert witness departs from objectivity of testimony at his or her own peril. The similarity between the expert witness and audit roles has recently been specifically acknowledged in revisions to the guidance on contingent fees (see Chapter 17).

If the special *status* of audit, and similar public financial reporting, is acknowledged as a peculiar element of the accountant's ethical regime, then *continuity* of appointment may be acceptable as another. Most legal work is assignment-based, and indeed such accountancy services as consultancy are also likely to be provided on an ad hoc basis. However audit – though determinable – has effectively a presumption of continuity, and tax compliance work (the bread and butter of most smaller practitioners) is also presumed to continue until there is a specific change of appointment (normally reflected in execution of a new tax agency mandate – the famous Form 64-8).

The requirement for all UK-registered companies, apart from the smallest, to have an auditor, and the probability that they will be assisted in relation to their taxation affairs by the audit firm, make it more rather than less likely that conflicts of interest will arise.

CONFLICTS OF INTEREST – AND THEIR MANAGEMENT

As has been indicated, the legal regulators are, very properly, particularly concerned to protect their members (and the latter's clients) from problems arising out of conflict of interest. Since a significant amount of legal work is *adversarial* in nature – that is, related to disputes between parties involving potentially legal action – the possibility that a legal firm might find itself acting for two opposing parties at the same time is to be avoided at all costs. Accordingly, requirements to withdraw from such situations as soon as they are identified are understandable, and probably essential.

It is also, of course, possible for a firm of accountants, acting for two business clients, to find itself in a situation where the interests of those clients clearly diverge: they may be bidding for the same property or enterprise; they may be trade competitors; they may both be seeking to take over a third enterprise, or one may be seeking to take over the other! However, the interests of neither – or any – of the parties may best be served by the auditors and long-term financial advisers withdrawing their services. Some might seek to argue that it is unconscionable that a member of a firm should continue to act for a predator organisation when a colleague is, possibly, possessed of material confidential information in relation to the target organisation. Few, however, would maintain that it is proper for the latter to have the advice and facilities of its auditors/accountants withdrawn precipitately and to be left to swim for itself in a shark-filled sea.

So the professional guidance has acknowledged, and indeed *recommends* measures to manage conflict in all but the most extreme situations. The detailed guidance in this area is explored in Chapter 10. It is perhaps worthwhile noting at this stage, however – before we confront the 'core' guidance on independence and objectivity – that the measures and safeguards identified include compartmentalisation of partners and teams, and regular review of the situation by a senior partner or compliance officer not personally involved with either client.

Topics for Discussion/Consideration

1 *Is it proper for the guidance for lawyers and that for accountants in relation to conflict of interest to differ so sharply – and does this not create great potential disruption for a 'team' of advisers (lawyers plus accountants) in, for example, takeover situations?*

2 *Anyone (with some expertise) can be engaged as an expert witness; but are there other roles in the non-accountancy professions which have an 'attest' element?*

3 *Would we like to see a greater use of 'attest' and 'assurance' on this side of the Atlantic?*

CHAPTER 5

Situations of possible threat to independence and objectivity

'INDEPENDENCE' IN THE DEVELOPED, 'TECHNICAL' SENSE

The rule books of all professional disciplines state a requirement for 'independence' on the part of their practitioners – but it is not always clear exactly what this means. In ethical guidance for accountants, independence has come to signify *the avoidance of situations which might threaten (or appear to threaten) objectivity*. The position is neatly summarised in the Statement (1.220) on the Ethical Responsibilities of Members in Business – which has to acknowledge, of course, that:

> the concept of independence ... has no direct relevance to the employed member ... Even for the practising accountant independence is not an end in itself: it is essentially a means of securing a more important end, namely an objective approach to work.

As we have seen, the ethical guidance for the accountancy profession, entitled until 1992 'Professional Independence', has sought to identify every potential threat to independence and hence objectivity. That means, in the terms of the recently issued Framework-based guidance – and indeed, of those of its immediate predecessor – the identification of *areas of threat or risk*.

The Framework was conceived as a possible route to avoiding highly detailed, proscriptive guidance on all manner of situations of perceived threat, and the Framework approach should indeed, in due course, make it possible to move towards shorter, more principle-based guidance. The reason for retention of all the previously identified areas of risk is explained later in this chapter. For the meantime, let us register two points:

1 The European body, FEE (Fédération des Experts Comptables et Economiques Européens) has accepted a 'position paper' on independence and objectivity, which acknowledges Framework principles and is currently on the
agenda of the new IFAC (International Federation of Accountants) Ethics Forum
– so the full potential significance of the Framework should not be forgotten.

2 Although the new, Framework-based Statement (1.201) does adopt the existing detailed list of areas of risk, it seeks to apply Framework principles (as we shall see) to those areas – and the detailed guidance follows a comprehensive introduction in which the Framework elements are carefully explained.

AREAS OF RISK

The reiteration of areas of risk in the latest Statement 1.201 is in much the same order as in the Statement just replaced, and is as follows:

- Undue dependence on an audit client.
- Loans to or from a client; guarantees; overdue fees.
- Hospitality or other benefits.
- Actual or threatened litigation.
- Other self-interest situations (participation in the affairs of a client; partner or senior employee joining client).
- Mutual business interest.
- Beneficial interest in shares and other investments.
- Beneficial interests in trusts.
- Trusteeships.
- Nominee shareholdings; 'bare trustee' shareholdings.
- Voting on audit appointments.
- Connections; associated firms; influences outside the practice: employees.
- Provision of other services to audit clients (including specialist valuations; over-familiarity; involvement in management).
- Acting for a prolonged period of time.

Readers who are not familiar with the previous Statement 1.201 may find it helpful to have a summary of the main considerations relating to each of the above identified areas of risk. References are to the Framework version of the Statement – which does not differ materially in content from the replaced version, although Framework terminology (see the next chapter) replaces most references to *perceived risks*.

Since one of the original objectives of the Framework was to move from guidance based on the empirical identification of all possible areas of risk to a more principle-based approach, the carrying over of these areas of risk into the new guidance warrants some explanation.

Part of the processes of the Chartered Accountants Joint Ethics Committee (CAJEC) is extensive, broad-based consultation. This is usually in two parts: an initial 'Green' Discussion Paper, and a subsequent 'White' Paper including an exposure draft of new guidance. It was in relation to the first, Green Discussion Paper on the Framework that a substantial ground swell of opinion manifested itself which acknowledged the advantages of the new approach, but expressed concern at the implications of removing the 'corset' represented by the existing identification of specific risk areas and situations. This ground swell included both smaller practitioner groups and the regulatory organs of the Institutes such as the Joint Monitoring Unit (JMU).

An additional reason for retention of the existing areas of risk, virtually in specie, was that moving the goalposts in any particular guidance area – for instance, by emitting a warning against a particular course of conduct – might produce particular hostility or approbation that would cloud the mandate – or absence of a mandate – for the Framework approach itself.

Accordingly, it was decided before the second consultation exercise on the Framework that the draft of new guidance exposed would maintain all the current provisions on particular situations.

Undue dependence on an audit client (4.1–4.9)

This area of risk relates to the threat to objectivity that arises when a firm receives recurring fees from a client company or group and those fees represent a proportion of the firm's overall fees which is unduly and dangerously high. Such guidance is a very common, if not universal, element in the guidance of accountancy bodies, usually incorporating a maximum figure or figures which cannot be exceeded with safety.

For many years the relevant overall maximum percentage has been, in the United Kingdom, 15 per cent. When the major revision of the Guide took place in 1990–92, a lower figure of 10 per cent was added in relation to listed or other public-interest companies. At the same time, the identification of the nature of the risk was broadened, and 'trigger points' of 10 per cent and 5 per cent respectively were added. These now appear under the heading of 'Safeguards'. The nub of the guidance is expressed in paragraph 4.2:

> **a member should not accept an audit appointment or similar financial reporting assignment from an entity which regularly provides him, his firm or an office within the firm with an unduly large proportion of his or its gross practice income.**

Exemptions are indicated in relation to new firms seeking to establish themselves, or established firms running down, 'at any event in the short term' (paragraph 4.4). Safeguards should be implemented where the limit is exceeded.

There is a warning that the fees from a collection of one-off assignments could contribute to 'a problem of undue dependence' and should be regarded 'on the same basis as recurring fees'.

The guidance, particularly in its latest form, emphasises that it is *dependence* which is at issue, not bare percentage figures. (Q/A3, at the end of Chapter 6, deals with a practical application of this guidance.)

Paragraphs 4.6 and 4.7 contain helpful advice on the personal threats which may arise to individual engagement partners, when review by another partner is likely to be a minimum safeguard.

Loans to or from a client; guarantees; overdue fees (4.10–4.14)

The provision or acceptance of a loan or guarantee in respect of a client will generally prevent a firm from acting or continuing as auditors. The same considerations apply to loans or guarantees provided to or by a principal in the firm.

Where the client is a financial institution, and a loan, overdraft or home mortgage is accepted by a principal or employee of the firm 'in the normal course of business and on normal commercial terms', the firm is normally able to report, unless:

(a) **the loan is applied so as to subscribe to partnership capital; or**
(b) **the principal is an engagement partner in relation to the client (paragraph 4.12).**

Significant overdue fees can have the same implications as a loan to a client (paragraph 4.13). Where fees are outstanding, the situation should be reviewed by an uninvolved principal before work is commenced on the audit (paragraph 4.14).

Hospitality or other benefits (4.15)

The guidance has for some years contained a warning against the acceptance of hospitality, etc., 'unless the value of any benefit is modest'. 'Modest' is not defined.

Actual or threatened litigation (4.16–4.19)

Guidance is provided in paragraphs 4.16–4.19 on the possible – but unlikely – situation of a client wishing a firm to continue as auditors when the two are locked into litigation with each other. Threats to objectivity can also arise in the course of 'third party' litigation if the firm should find itself having to allege fraud or deceit against an audit client. The same paragraph (4.18) provides some leeway for a firm's continuing to act 'when the litigation arises solely out of a fee dispute'.

Other self-interest situations (participation in the affairs of a client; partner or senior employee joining client) (4.20–4.29)

Participation in a client's undertaking is likely to constitute an unacceptable threat to objectivity. That is almost too obvious to require stating. Paragraphs 4.55–4.78 of the Statement confront the possibility of the participation arising in the course of the provision of other services to an audit client (see Chapter 7).

The guidance which features under the above heading relates effectively to participation by members of the firm in the undertaking of a client *in a managerial capacity*, and vice versa, together with the possibility of recruitment by the client of someone connected with the firm, and the converse. (Q/A1 and Q/A2 at the end of Chapter 6 deal with some practical applications of paragraph 4.23 – close connections of a principal of the audit firm.)

So far as an officer or employee of an audit client joining the audit firm is concerned, the guidance (paragraph 4.24) requires 'two years of clear water under the bridge' before the transferor can personally take part in the conduct of the audit of that client.

Assistance to a company secretary

If any principal of the firm were to hold office as secretary of an audit client company, that would constitute a breach of Section 27 of the Companies Act 1989. The guidance, however, goes considerably further than this, to the extent of advising that: 'A firm should not report on a company if a company associated with the firm fills the appointment of secretary to the company.' Firms have sometimes been inclined to interpret the words 'associated with the firm' rather narrowly! (See Q/A5 at the end of Chapter 6.)

It should be noted (paragraph 4.25) that the objection is to accepting appointment as company secretary, not *providing assistance* to the company secretary. The provision of such assistance to the secretaries of smaller companies, in relation to filing requirements and so on, is a well-established feature of the service expected from audit firms.

Partner or senior employee joining client

This section of the guidance on other self interest situations was only introduced a couple of years ago. It does not appear to have caused any difficulties in that short time. The main guidance warnings (paragraph 4.27 (a)/(b)) relate to possible pressure on the partner/senior employee's former firm arising from the existence of retirement and pension benefits or continuing ostensible links, such as inclusion of the former member's name on firm's literature, or continuing provision by the firm of accommodation or support.

This is an instance where – no doubt because of its recent creation – the existing guidance required very little modification to accord with Framework principles, with safeguards already featuring prominently. Safeguards such as those quoted in this section of guidance in particular do have the air of *technical* guidance rather than ethical. This is one of a number of indications that the traditional gap between the technical guidance of the bodies and the Guide to Professional Ethics is shrinking – and in certain areas disappearing altogether. Another is the inclusion in such documents as 'The Audit Agenda' of specific ethical requirements such as independence and objectivity, and references to change in a professional appointment.

Mutual business interest (4.30)

This is another area of risk which is very clear and obvious. Although the possibility of implementing 'appropriate safeguards' is indicated in the Statement, there can be little doubt that the existence of a substantial mutual business interest with an audit client is essentially incompatible with the audit/reporting roles.

Beneficial interests in shares and other investments (4.31–4.38)

It is the established position, on both sides of the Atlantic, that *any* direct beneficial interest in a client organisation is incompatible with auditing or reporting upon it. There is no de minimis exemption.

Because of considerations previously referred to, the Framework-based guidance maintains this traditional position. Accordingly, the guidance continues to focus on drawing the line in relation to such 'marginal' investments as unit trusts or Lloyd's syndicates holding shares in audit client companies (which are permitted) and PEPs (which are generally not permitted – because the PEPs legislation requires *direct* shareholdings).

It is arguable – and no doubt will be argued in the future – that the outlawing of even insignificant direct beneficial interests in an audit client is not consistent with Framework principles – because if the holding is insignificant in value, the threat is likely to be insignificant in fact. If a time ever comes when such arguments are taken seriously, then an extraordinarily difficult drafting problem will arise – the definition of 'significant'!

However, the only exception indicated in the guidance (paragraph 4.38) to the uncompromising prohibition of such interests stated above is in relation to those companies where the auditor is required to be a shareholder, either by statute (which must be increasingly rare) or by the articles of association of, for example, a sporting or social organisation. Even where, in the case of such sporting or social bodies, there is not an actual requirement for the auditor to be a member, there is something like an 'understanding' that the Investigation Committees of the bodies are unlikely to proceed against the auditor of a golf club or local charity who is an 'ordinary' member of the body and is required, as a condition of membership, to hold a single qualifying share or provide a stipulated minimum guarantee. The overt reason for this unique, unofficial exemption is presumably to avoid denying the delights or virtues of membership of such bodies to professional accountants. There must, however, be some sort of matching, implicit assumption that such minimal shareholdings or guarantees *do* only represent an insignificant threat to objectivity – and this may prove to be the acorn from which oaks will eventually spring!

It should be noted that the prohibition only extends to principals in the firm and their connections. Where the beneficial interest is that of an employee, the guidance restriction is on the latter taking part in the audit of the company (paragraph 4.32).

Beneficial interests in trusts (4.39–4.41)

Where a principal in a firm, or a close connection of the principal, is a beneficiary in a trust which owns shares in an audit client, the guidance indicates that similar considerations to those relating to a direct beneficial interest in the company apply. However, the prohibition on the firm's acting is restricted to those circumstances in which the holder of the beneficial interest is the principal or anyone closely connected with him or her *and* the principal is also the relevant trustee. If the beneficiary/principal is not a trustee, he or she is only required to 'cease personally to take part in the audit of the company' (paragraph 4.41).

Trusteeships (4.42–4.47)

The guidance of the UK bodies is comparatively liberal in regard to situations where a firm, or a principal or employee of the firm, acts as a trustee of a trust holding shares in an audit client company. The guidance does not include any blanket prohibition against the firm continuing to report, and those prohibitions which do exist may be summarised as follows. The Firm should not continue to audit:

1 Where the trust holds shares in a listed company or other public-interest company, and

(a) the holding is in excess of 10 per cent of the issued share capital (paragraphs 4.43 and 4.44 contain aggregation provisions), or

(b) the value of the shareholding is in excess of 10 per cent of the total assets of the trust (paragraph 4.43).

2 In any case where the trustee (or the trustee's close connection) is the audit engagement partner in respect of the company.

A rigid application of the final criterion would mean, of course, that sole practitioners would be unable to accept trustee appointments in relation to trusts which include shares in audit client companies. When the Guide was reviewed in 1990–92 concern was expressed on behalf of sole practitioners, and accordingly there is an 'out' for them – consultation with another member (paragraph 4.46(b)).

Nominee shareholdings; 'bare trustee' shareholdings (4.48)

These are to be treated on the same basis as trustee shareholdings (above).

Voting on audit appointments (4.49)

It will be apparent from the previous four items that principals or (more probably) employees may find themselves holding shares in an audit client company. The Guide to Professional Ethics has for many years provided, at this point, that such shares should not be voted in relation to the appointment, removal or remuneration of auditors. The latest, Framework-based guidance comments that to vote such shares 'would give rise to a patent conflict of interest'. It could therefore be argued that this guidance would be more appropriately sited in the Statement (1.204) on Conflicts of Interest.

Connections; associated firms; influences outside the practice; employees (4.50–4.54)

This is something of a 'wrap-up' section, which both co-ordinates and extends the previous guidance. Close connections have been referred to already in connection with paragraph 4.23 ('Participation in the affairs of a client'), and will feature again in relation to paragraph 4.54 (Q/A2 at the end of Chapter 6). The guidance in this area is summarised in Chapter 7 (qv).

The essence of the guidance on connections and influences is that:

each of the threats dealt with in paragraphs 2.1–4.49 may arise *either in relation to a principal of the firm, or in relation to a close connection such as a member of his immediate family … (or) because of pressures exerted upon a* *firm by an associated firm or an outside source introducing business.* (paragraph 4.50) (emphasis added)

Further advice on the considerations which apply is given in paragraph 4.51. All the safeguards listed in the Introduction are 'of potential relevance', and factors for consideration include:

● closeness of relationships and associations;
● the strength of an associate's interest in the firm's retaining the client; and
● the extent to which the introduction of business by an outside source is able to affect the firm's fee income.

Provision of other services to audit clients (including specialist valuations); over-familiarity; involvement in management) (4.55–4.78)

This is another area which is dealt with in detail in Chapter 7 (qv). As we have seen, the need to address on a more consistent basis the provision of other services to audit clients was very close to the origin of the Framework, and is the section of guidance which best illustrates the application of Framework principles. It should be noted, in relation to the provision of *specialist valuations* for audit clients – which are generally 'prohibited' – that the temporary exemption in respect of actuarial valuations, indicated in 1993, continues, because their particular situation is still proving difficult to resolve.

Acting for a prolonged period of time (4.79–4.83)

This is another area considered in more detail in Chapter 7. It is an area where, although the substantive guidance has changed not at all, incorporation within the Framework is likely to create some additional, compliance-type duties for firms.

'PROHIBITED' SITUATIONS

Traditionally, some of the above areas of risk have been regarded as imposing so significant a threat to, in particular, *audit* objectivity that the practitioner has no option but to decline to accept or continue appointment. This is still so under the Framework-based guidance, even if the auditor genuinely believes that the circumstances are such that available safeguards and procedures could, in his or her particular case, enable him or her to maintain proper objectivity. For convenience the term 'prohibition' is sometimes used, in this chapter and elsewhere, in relation to these areas of risk, where 'warning against ...' would be literally more correct. The above summary indicates that the situations which are effectively 'prohibited' include the following:

- Loans to or from a client (with exceptions in the case of loans, overdrafts or home mortgages accepted from an audit client financial institution in the normal course of business and on normal commercial terms).
- Litigation – where a writ for negligence has been issued by the client against the auditor.
- Participation in the affairs of a client: partner, or close connection, as officer or senior employee.
- A substantial mutual business interest.
- Direct beneficial interest in the client.
- Trusteeship where there is a significant shareholding in a listed or public-interest client.
- Provision of other services: participation in the preparation of the accounts/ accounting records of listed or public-interest clients.
- Specialist valuations where provided to an audit client.
- Involvement in management of a client.

A firm's acceptance or continuance of an audit appointment in any of the above circumstances would, on the basis of pre-Framework guidance, almost inevitably result in reference to the investigation/disciplinary processes of the bodies. CAJEC and the bodies have, as we have seen, acknowledged explicitly that implementation of the new Framework-based Statement will not for the time being 'move the goalposts' in relation to any areas of risk, including those where an appointment was previously regarded as unacceptable.

The above summary is necessarily terse, and the relevant provisions in the new Statement 1.201 need to be studied in detail in every case. It has in earlier chapters been emphasised that the ethical regime affecting UK accountants is based on guidance rather than regulation, with the implication that a member or firm should be able to argue that a guidance warning should not apply in the particular circumstances of his or her case. In relation to the above circumstances, however, members have been uniformly unsuccessful in persuading disciplinary tribunals that this should be so. Paragraph 3.9 of the new Statement 1.201 is relevant in this respect:

> **there are some situations in which the threat to an auditor's objectivity is so significant, or generally perceived to be so, that an auditor should, having regard to preservation of the public image of his profession, decline to accept appointment, even if he believes that the circumstances are such that available safeguards and procedures could, in his particular case, enable him to**

maintain proper objectivity. In this eventuality, he should decline or resign appointment.

The situations listed should be presumed to be included among those indicated in this quoted passage.

It will become apparent from the next chapter that, as well as the above situations which could be described fairly as 'no go', there will be particular circumstances in which the risks are too great, and/or the 'available safeguards and procedures' insufficiently effective, for a member to accept or continue appointment. The new Statement draws on and applies Framework principles to enable a decision to be reached as to whether it is safe and proper to accept and proceed in each particular case. The next chapter will, in addition to summarising the Framework approach, also focus in a question-and-answer section on particular situations of interest such as 'the Marks and Spencer scenario'.

STRUCTURE OF THE STATEMENT

In the meantime, it is probably appropriate to record that the new Statement is, like Caesar's Gaul (and indeed the predecessor Statement), divided into three parts (supplemented by a definitions section):

Section A – Objectivity, Independence and Audit

Section B – Objectivity and Independence in Financial Reporting and Similar Non-Audit Roles

Section C – Independence in Professional Roles Other than those Covered in Sections A and B.

Independence and financial reporting in non-audit roles

The areas of risk which we have been considering all feature in Section A of Statement 1.201, and are phrased throughout in terms of audit appointments. Sections B and C of the Statement then go on to consider the extent to which the Areas of Risk occur in non-audit situations.

(It has been argued that it would be both more logical and user-friendly for this core Statement to proceed from the general to the particular, rather than vice versa. The justifications for the current approach include the following:

1 The special status of audit, and the significance that objectivity and independence bear in relation to it (previously considered).

2 The need for the guidance on audit to be as specific in terminology in relation to audit situations as possible.

3 The fact that new ethical guidance on 'Independence and the Audit' was a prerequisite of the recognition of the professional bodies in respect of audit regulation (August 1991).)

Section B of the Statement issued in February 1992 dealt simply, and for the most part clearly, with 'financial reporting and similar non-audit roles' by providing that 'the considerations referred to in Section A … apply'! The effect is that all the guidance warnings and prohibitions contained in Section A apply, *mutatis mutandis*, to the following roles:

● financial reporting assignments requiring a professional opinion (other than reports for management's internal use only) (paragraphs 5.2–5.3);
● litigation support, including expert witness work and 'forensic accounting' (paragraph 5.4);
● specialist valuations (which as we have seen should not, in general, be provided to audit clients) (paragraph 5.5);
● when acting as an arbitrator (paragraph 5.6); and
● (an addition) due diligence work, as defined and dealt with in Statement 1.203 (anticipated to be approved by the bodies in Autumn 1996).

Independence in other professional roles – Section C

Some of these (non-audit/non-reporting) roles are listed in paragraph 6.1:

● taxation services;
● preparation of accounts;
● corporate advisory services other than the preparation of documents for public use;
● management consultancy services; and
● reporting to management/secondment to management.

The areas of risk referred to earlier do not necessarily apply to these roles. However (paragraph 6.2), objectivity must not be impaired, and conflicts of interest (Statement 1.204) should not be ignored. Three particular areas of risk are selected for mention:

1 *Family and other personal relationships* These provisions (paragraphs 6.4–6.5) are somewhat abbreviated, compared with the previous guidance. In accordance with the Framework approach, the self-interest and familiarity threats are emphasised, and certain safeguards indicated, including disclosure.

2 *Loans*   Firms and their principals are still warned against making loans to, or receiving loans from a client. There is, however, a somewhat broader exemption in relation to loans accepted from client financial institutions (paragraph 6.8) than in the case of Section A and B roles, in the same terms as the previous guidance, and overdue fees are again identified as subject to similar considerations.

3 *Goods and services: hospitality or other benefits*   The warning here is identical to that in Section A.

Beneficial interests and investments in Section C clients

This guidance is also 'as before', save for inclusion of a reference to self-interest threats (see next chapter). Investments in clients not reported upon are permitted – subject to safeguards and 'materiality' – and a member acting as a 'business adviser to a client' may invest in, sponsor or promote its shares, subject to such safeguards as are appropriate to the particular case, including disclosure of the relationship to relevant parties.

Section D – definitions

The definitions which appeared formerly at the end of Section A now form a new definitions section at the end of the Statement. Since – in recognition of the growth of corporate practices – the word 'principal' generally replaces the former 'partner' in the text of the Statement, a definition of 'Principal' is now included.

Topics for Discussion/Consideration

1 *The IFAC Code for Professional Accountants (qv) is in two sections, the first (which includes some 'independence' provisions) applicable to all accountants, whether in practice or not. (The second section applies only to members in practice.) Is there sufficient community of interest and position between the various strands of the profession for such a first section to be meaningful?*

2 *Is audit so different a role from any other – inside or outside the accountancy profession – that there should be a special 'code' for audits?*

CHAPTER 6

The Framework approach – risks and safeguards

THE FRAMEWORK

For the last chapter or two, the Framework has been waiting in the wings – the subject of advance previews, hints and other references of the kind associated with forthcoming attractions.

The arrival of the Framework is also overdue in another sense: it is now nearly three years since the Framework was first conceived , the overlong gestation period between conception and birth/christening being due partly to the need to re-express the original Framework document in a more concise and specific form, suitable for embodiment in the Guide to Professional Ethics of the three UK and Irish Institutes, coupled with the extensive – but time-consuming – processes of widespread consultation undertaken by CAJEC (the Chartered Accountants Joint Ethics Committee) before new guidance is submitted to the Institutes.

This is not, perhaps, the place for retelling in detail the full story of the development of the Framework. It was, in summary, first conceived by Brian Currie, at the request of the then President of ICAEW in the context of the anxieties earlier referred to about the way in which the guidance on independence and objectivity was going: the identification of more and more areas of potential perceived risk in a perhaps peremptory and ad hoc manner, in the absence of any cogent and persuasive rationale or principles.

The first, and perhaps most important conclusion reached by Brian Currie was that it was unrealistic to think of a professional regime free from any actual or perceived threats to objectivity; all professional 'deciders' (to use the Currie term) are faced with threats to their objectivity – starting with the threat that the professional is paid by the client and presumably wishes to go on being paid. That appreciation led to another conclusion: that the first purpose of professional guidance should be to enable the practitioner to identify the threats and risks affecting his or her situation, so that these could be addressed.

The only way in which the threats could be so addressed would be by the employment of appropriate and acknowledged safeguards. The professional guidance should also seek to assist the practitioner to identify and apply these.

The final step in the process would be for the practitioner (with assistance if necessary) to weigh the safeguards against the threats, to enable him or her to decide whether it was safe and proper to accept or continue the appointment which had produced the threat situation.

So, the Framework is essentially an approach, process or technique whereby:

1 the threats implicit in a situation are identified;
2 safeguards which may properly be employed to negate or reduce those threats are also identified; and
3 safeguards are then weighed against threats, threats against safeguards, to reach a decision as to whether objectivity is sufficiently assured and protected for the practitioner to proceed.

Proponents of 'Independence' as a concept might seek to add at the end of item 3, 'in the knowledge that his independence is accordingly assured'. However, the new approach focuses primarily upon *objectivity* (a state of mind – which learned judges have said can be just as much a matter of fact as the state of one's digestion!), instead of on *independence*, which is either:

● an abstract concept, or
● another way of saying 'the avoidance of situations which threaten objectivity'.

Thus the Framework is with us at last. What are the practical implications?

Well, the most important physical implication is that we now have a Statement (1.201) on integrity, objectivity and independence, which seeks to provide practical help for practitioners in the identification of risks and threats and the application of safeguards in reaching a proper conclusion as to whether it is safe to act. Although the introductory paragraphs of the Statement deal with these elements in some detail, it may be appropriate to summarise them here.

THE THREATS

Before listing the threats themselves, one should, perhaps, return to what amounts to Brian Currie's words on the principles behind their categorisation:

It may prove helpful to members to categorise the threats because the more clearly the nature of the threat is identified, the clearer it becomes

● **whether the member's own integrity and working environment may be sufficient to offset/mitigate the threat,**
● **whether specific safeguards should be added,**

- if safeguards should be added, which of those would most appropriately address the risk,
- in what circumstances the appearance of risk or conflict becomes so great that there ought to be an absolute requirement such as a prohibition.

(Paragraph 1.6 of the new Statement)

This section of the Introduction to 1.201 goes on to confront the possible criticisms of those who would cry 'Withdraw! Withdraw!' as soon as a threat is identified:

This could however deny to clients proper access to the member's breadth of professional expertise and knowledge of the client's business, and, in deciding whether to include such a prohibition in its guidance, the Institute always bears in mind the need to maintain a balance that respects the interests of clients and the possible wider public interest.

Five 'basic' threats are identified:

1 The self-interest threat (e.g. the desire to retain a client).
2 The self-review threat (e.g. when seeking to report on one's own, or a partner's assessment).
3 The advocacy threat: a (conceivably emotional) commitment to the client's position when one has been involved in 'arguing the client's corner' in an adversarial situation.
4 The familiarity or trust threat: becoming over-influenced by the personalities and qualities of the client's management.
5 The initimidation threat: over-influence from fear (of the client or another).

In the course of consultation, additional threats have been put forward. They have, however, on close analysis, proved to be aspects of one or other of the five threats listed above.

SAFEGUARDS TO OFFSET THE THREATS

Neither safeguards as a concept, nor the specific list of safeguards in the recently issued guidance, are new. The safeguards and procedures, including those arising from the environment of the practice or of the profession itself, which occupy several pages in the Statement – paragraphs 3.2 to 3.9 – will already be largely familiar to those within the profession (although it is helpful to be reminded, no doubt). Non-accountants should find them a valuable aid in understanding the culture of the profession. The specific steps which may be taken by firms by way of safeguard include establishment of internal procedures for training and communication, review arrangements with a partner or qualified colleague, rotation of staff or engagement partners, and other elements, making up:

> **An overall control environment, starting with a professional approach towards matters of quality and ethics, and taking in staff training, development and performance appraisal, and the assurance provided by a regularly monitored and evidenced control system.**

The guidance follows its predecessor in going into some detail on the review arrangements appropriate to sole practitioners and small firms. (A sole-practitioner registered auditor is already required to indicate standing arrangements for external review.)

The final expressed 'safeguard' (3.9) may or may not amount to a safeguard like the others. It is nevertheless 'fail-safe': it is 'refusal to act where no other course can abate the perceived problem'!

In addition to the general sections on both threats and safeguards included in paragraphs 2.0 to 3.10 of the Statement, detailed analysis of threats and safeguards accompanies most of the guidance on specific situations, which was summarised in the preceding chapter. The most detailed application of threats and safeguards is in relation to the provision of other services to audit clients (paragraphs 4.55–4.78). In particular, extensive guidance on the *advocacy* threat occurs in paragraphs 4.67–4.73. 'Other services' will receive more consideration in the next chapter.

Relevant Queries

Q1 *Can I audit my brother/sister-in-law's company?*

A1 'Brothers and sisters and their spouses' are added to the definition of 'closely connected' persons so far as their being an officer or senior employee of an audit client is concerned. The implication is that it would be wrong for the enquirer's firm to audit in those circumstances.

Q2 *(The 'Marks and Spencer scenario') The London office of our firm audits a huge national retailer. The student daughter of the tax manager of our Aberdeen Office has a holiday job with the retailer. What, if anything, should we do?*

A2 The guidance of paragraph 4.54 of Statement 1.201 advises that 'the threat to objectivity will be less where any connection is with a junior member of staff or with a member of the firm who is not personally engaged on the audit in question, where his or her office is distant from the office conducting the audit, and where effective safeguards are in place in the internal procedures of the firm'. The scenario outlined in this question is at the other end of the 'connection spectrum' from the previous question. No one could reasonably diagnose a threat – presumably it could only (theoretically) be a familiarity threat – to the objectivity of the reporting partner.

Q3 *The guidance of paragraph 4.2 of Statement 1.201 advises that a member should not accept an audit appointment from an entity which regularly provides him, his firm or an office within the firm with a proportion of gross practice income of 15 per cent or more. On the other hand, there is some sort of exemption (4.4) for a firm running up or running down – provided indicated safeguards are implemented. I am a sole practitioner, and derive 26 per cent of my fees from a small group of companies. What should I do?*

A3 An external review is indicated as a relevant safeguard in paragraph 4.8. However, the percentage is so far above the 'limit' in your case that you are vulnerable to the argument that your objectivity must almost certainly be affected. You could, of course, demonstrate or protect your objectivity by withdrawing from certain roles – in particular, the reporting role. Where the Joint Monitoring Unit (JMU) becomes aware of this sort of situation, it will normally ask the member to seek advice from his or her Institute's ethical advisory services. The JMU inspector will, no doubt, re-examine the problem on a subsequent visit. If the proportion is showing a downward tendency, then the member will probably receive sympathetic consideration. If, however, the proportion is so high, and growing, then the JMU will probably draw the matter formally to the attention of the relevant Institute.

Q4 *Paragraph 4.15 of Statement 1.201 only requires, in relation to 'hospitality or other benefits' that 'the value of any benefit is modest'! What is meant by 'modest' in this connection?*

A4 This particular section of guidance has always caused drafting problems, and the current terminology is, of course, something of a compromise. It may be easier to recognise when hospitality, in particular, is *immodest* or *excessive*. For example, the acceptance of a loan of a client's villa in Monte Carlo, or his forty-foot Mediterranean yacht for two weeks could hardly be regarded as 'modest' in value in the appreciation of any ordinary mortal. However, a bottle of malt whisky at Christmas, particularly if reciprocated, is unlikely to shock anybody's sensibilities!

Q5 *The guidance (paragraph 4.25) advises that a firm should not report on a company 'if a company associated with the firm fills the appointment of secretary to the company'. The partners in our firm have, in fact, set up a* *little company of which their wives are directors and shareholders. Would there be any objection to that company accepting office as company secretary of our clients, including audit clients?*

A5 The Ethics Committees of the accountancy bodies in the United Kingdom have steadfastly advised that this would represent 'association', such as to prevent the firm reporting. If the officers of the client company were, corporately, guilty of some misfeasance or nonfeasance the threat to the objectivity of the reporting partner would be patent, and even if the company secretary were not 'personally' involved, there is a clear self-interest element in the firm's turning a blind eye. It is unlikely that even a bachelor partner could demonstrate his objectivity in such circumstances. This is probably a good example of 'situations in which the threat to an auditor's objectivity is so significant ... that [he] should, having regard to preservation of the public image of his profession, decline to accept appointment' (paragraph 3.9).

CHAPTER 7

Differences in guidance arising from the new Framework-based Statement

This chapter will examine three different areas of the guidance on integrity, objectivity and independence which have been subject to particular revision under the new Statement: 'Other services', where the new guidance is very much more extensive; 'Connections', which now feature in three rather than two sections of the Statement; and the section previously headed 'Rotation of audit partners', where the appearance and location of the guidance have changed to some extent but the substantive provisions are hardly changed at all. This chapter will also examine the extra flexibility in many areas vouchsafed by the Framework approach, but also the *quid pro quo*: a new need to document that Framework procedures – of identification and 'weighing' – have taken place in relation to all relevant assignments, and that the safeguards identified as appropriate have in fact been implemented.

OTHER SERVICES

The extent to which an audit firm should be able to supply ancillary services to audit clients has, for a number of years, preoccupied both the profession and the media. One of the reasons why this is so is the different positions that have been adopted in relation to other services by the Anglo-Saxon accountancy profession and by the Continental accountancy regulators. As we have seen, in the United Kingdom and United States in particular, a range of other services – from taxation advice to a constantly increasing variety of consultancy services, including IT systems design and implementation, increasing involvement in corporate finance activities, including most recently the role of 'sponsor' under the London Stock Exchange's latest Listing Rules, and litigation support – could properly be provided to audit clients, subject only to the warning that those other services should not involve:

1 participation in the accounting records of a listed or public interest body, or

2 involvement in management action or decisions.

The provision of specialist valuations to audit clients has, since 1993, been the subject of specific, prohibitory guidance, although the particular case of actuarial valuations was exempted to allow further consideration to take place. That consideration has not yet been concluded, and the new Statement is issued with the same 'temporary' exemption in respect of actuarial valuations.

The debate on 'other services' dates back to before the 1978 Report of the Cohen Commission in the United States – a long time in accountancy ethics. Nevertheless it is still to the Cohen Commission Report that supporters of the provision of 'other services' ultimately refer – and to the Report's conclusion that there was no evidence that the quality or validity of audit had been adversely affected.

Since the guidance has – with the exception of specialist valuations – consisted of *warnings* about the boundaries of acting, rather than 'prohibition', the flexibility of the Framework approach should be particularly relevant. There will be some circumstances in which the safeguards attaching to the provision of a particular service to a particular client will not be adequate to counter the threats; there will be other combinations of circumstances where the firm may reasonably conclude that the safeguards are adequate. The section in the new Statement on 'other services' is the longest, apart from the Introduction, but it is of significance to virtually every audit firm – whether it has only small audit clients, whom it assists with the preparation of accounts, and with taxation compliance and advice, or whether it is a large firm with many listed clients for whom the amount disclosed in the accounts for the provision of additional services by the auditor exceeds the audit fee itself, perhaps by a factor of 1.5:1.

Other services in detail

The first thing to appreciate about the new guidance is that it is 'ordered' by relevant *threats* rather than *services*. That is not necessarily the case in relation to other areas of risk, and, in any event, the detailed application of the threats is much more extensive here than elsewhere in the Statement. Indeed, this section of the Statement provides the best practical examples of the analysis-of-threats element in the Framework process.

The section commences with the identification of the provision of other services to audit clients as an 'area of risk', to which all the safeguards featured in the introduction may apply, and follows this with both a justification of the general value of the facility to provide other services and a warning about performing management functions or making management decisions. Nothing surprising so far!

It is in the paragraphs from 4.58–4.74 that the detailed exposition of threats in relation to the provision of various, specified services takes place. Sometimes the validity of particular safeguards is indicated. More often, it is the ultimate safeguard – of ceasing to act where the involvement of the firm is at the 'red end' of the 'spectrum' – that is indicated. At its conclusion the section features a further warning on 'involvement in management', where all the listed threats to objectivity could be aroused.

It may be helpful to indicate 'milestones' to assist the reader through this long section, although these do not, of course, represent an alternative to studying the guidance in detail.

Area of risk – provision of other services to audit clients

4.55–4.57   Identification of area of risk – all safeguards potentially relevant – provision of other services assists knowledge of a client's business and is therefore a 'good thing'; *contra*, performing management functions or making management decisions.

4.58   **Self-interest threat**

The perceived financial self-interest threat which relates to all work is increased by work or services additional to the audit – need to relate back to guidance on undue dependence.

4.59–4.64   **Self-review threat**

(a) Audit itself involves review of one's prior-year judgements, which the provision of other services augments (e.g. design/ recommendation of systems/controls relevant to the audit). Possible safeguard, 'compartmentalisation' between systems team and audit team.

(b) Preparation of accounting records creates a 'spectrum of involvement' by the auditor – even in case of a major listed company there will be some auditor-involvement (e.g. correcting omissions). Safeguards are necessary: at smaller company end, a considered analysis by the auditor of his or her involvement; in case of listed/public-interest company, firms should not participate in preparation of accounts/accounting records save for routine 'clerical' work (e.g. finalisation of statutory accounts/ consolidations/tax provisions, or emergency assistance). Need for regular review of scale and nature of work.

4.65–4.66   **Specialist valuations**

(a) As an example of self-review threat.

(b) 'Prohibition' on their provision.

4.67–4.73 Advocacy threat

(a) Firm entitled to support its clients' interests, but this must not affect the objectivity of the 'true and fair view'. Some advocacy roles, adopted objectively, may progressively commit the auditor's mind to the client's cause.

(b) Particular danger areas:
   (i) recommendation/promotion/underwriting of shares;
   (ii) leading corporate finance team which takes responsibility for (i);
   (iii) adoption of 'an extreme position' *re* accounting principles, taxation, and so on – possible safeguards: recommendation of alternate advisers for adversarial advocacy; in certain cases, compartmentalisation.

4.74 Over-familiarity threat

Dangers of being progressively drawn into management sphere.

4.75–4.78 Involvement in management (all threats)

(a) 'Prohibited' if management decisions involved.

(b) Particular situations of potential danger:
   (i) long-term advice to management;
   (ii) design of operating systems – safeguards: second opinion, management's own expertise, compartmentalisation;
   (iii) recruitment of key staff.

(c) Final decisions must be left to management in all cases.

CLOSE CONNECTIONS – 'FAMILY AND OTHER PERSONAL RELATIONSHIPS' (TITLE OF FORMER GUIDANCE)

This is an area where a little (prior) learning may be a dangerous thing! Readers who were not particularly familiar with the preceding guidance, and the section entitled 'Family and other personal relationships', should find no difficulty in coming to terms with the new Statement in which the significance of persons connected with a practice, or an individual in a practice, is set out more comprehensively. Those, however, accustomed to the 'old' guidance (where family, personal and business relationships with clients were lumped together) may find themselves searching around.

The 'tone' on *connections* is established in paragraph 2.6 of the introductory section to the new Statement, where the suggestion that 'connections and relationships' should constitute a separate 'threat' is considered, and disposed of:

Each of the above threats may arise either in relation to the auditor's own person or in relation to a connected person such as a member of his family or a partner or person who is close to him for some other reason, such as past or present association or obligation or indebtedness.

That principle is set out in terms in paragraph 4.50 of the new Statement, cross-referenced to the definition of 'closely connected' which is adopted, word for word, from the previous guidance.

Paragraph 4.54 repeats the major part of the previous guidance dealing with what we have called earlier 'the Marks and Spencer scenario' (see in particular the questions section at the end of Chapter 6). The other principal change in this part of the guidance is that the elements of the old section 'Family and other personal relationships' now feature as:

1 *Participation in the affairs of a client* (paragraphs 4.20–4.25, with the previous reference to 'close connections' embodied in paragraph 4.23).
2 *Mutual business interest* (paragraph 4.30).

The changes are not thought materially to alter the application of the guidance.

ACTING FOR A PROLONGED PERIOD OF TIME

That last rider applies also to the guidance which is now entitled as above, but which previously featured as 'Rotation of audit partners'. 'Rotation' is not, of course, an area of risk, but a *safeguard*. As such, it is located in the introductory section to the new Statement, paragraph 3.5 (iii). Substantively there should be no change.

However, the reframing of this guidance does constitute a good example of the potential additional duties for firms arising from the Framework process.

THE NEED TO RECORD CONSIDERATION OF THREATS AND SAFEGUARDS

As was indicated at the beginning of this chapter, the new Framework-based approach and guidance Statement should give more flexibility to firms in deciding whether or not they are able to act in those situations which have not been identified as fundamentally incompatible with audit and equivalent financial reporting roles. 'Following the spirit of the guidance' can now be equated with following Framework principles. If a firm can demonstrate that it has gone through the process of identification of threats, of evaluation of safeguards, and of weighing the latter against the former to decide whether it is safe and proper to proceed, then if the conclusion is a reasonably responsible one, the firm should not be vulnerable to investigation/discipline. That is, of course, providing that *the firm is also able to demonstrate that the relevant safeguards have been implemented*.

The guidance now entitled 'Area of risk – acting for a prolonged period of time' offers, as has been indicated, a good example of the potential application of this process, that is:

1 Multi-partner firms should have procedures designed to ensure that no audit engagement partner remains in charge of the audit of a listed company for a period exceeding seven consecutive years.
2 Sole-practitioner auditors of listed companies need to be able to demonstrate that they have:
   (a) carried out their own internal review, at least annually, of the file, and, if such a course is then indicated,
   (b) implemented the standing arrangements for external consultation (see paragraph 3.7).
   Presumably external consultation will always be required where the sole-practitioner has been the auditor for a period of more than seven consecutive years.
3 Whenever a renewal of audit appointment requires some reassurance that audit objectivity has been observed, firms should carry out a similar review. (That is the apparent effect of paragraph 3.6(i).)
4 The review requirement in relation to item 3 above also exists 'in respect of senior audit staff' (see paragraph 4.83).

Clearly, if a firm wishes to rest easy, it should provide for an annual review in relation to every audit appointment. Further, 'It is useful practice to keep records of all reviews carried out' (paragraph 3.6(iii)). But so far as 'statutory' audits are concerned, the firm is allowed no discretion whatever: recently imposed, tougher Audit Regulations (ICAEW, ICAS, ICAI) contain a specific provision (AR 3.04) that : 'A Registered Auditor must consider its independence and ability to perform the audit properly and record this before it accepts appointment or reappointment as auditor.'

Note: The Chartered Association (ACCA) has not, as yet, adopted this section of guidance.

These are, of course, very early days so far as interpretation of the new

Statement is concerned. The consultation document that introduced the exposure draft of the Statement in Spring 1995, promised that the Statement would be further developed, in accordance with Framework Principles, one aim being a more succinct document, in which principle rather than detail was emphasised. In addition, CAJEC has promised that the Guide will be reviewed in its entirety, from the point of view of reformulation along Framework lines where appropriate. The three Statements which follow 1.201, being mainly about objectivity, are accordingly ripe for review. They will be considered over the next three chapters, commencing with the Statement on Insolvency Practice. Readers are however asked to remind themselves periodically that these Statements are still in pre-Framework form.

Relevant Queries

Q1 *References to special requirements in respect of 'listed companies' (e.g. in the guidance on undue dependence, paragraphs 4.1–4.9) lump them in with 'other public interest companies', as defined. Rotation of the audit engagement partner is effectively mandatory, at least every seven years, for a firm's listed-client companies. Does this apply also to public-interest companies and organisations?*

A1 No. The requirements for 'mandatory' rotation were deliberately restricted to listed companies only. For all other bodies they are recommended – but a matter of discretion for the firm.

Q2 *How about rotation of the 'independent accountant' role, which is an alternative to audit for smaller companies?*

A2 The guidance of Section B of the Statement effectively makes the independent accountant subject to the same provisions as an auditor.

CHAPTER 8

The ethics of insolvency practice

A GUIDANCE STATEMENT WHICH IS REGULATORY IN TONE

We have considered in earlier chapters the arguments for and against guidance as opposed to regulations as the basis of a profession's ethical regime, together with the search by the Anglo-Saxon accountancy profession for principles and the 'moral high ground', rather than detailed, quasi-regulatory guidance or 'rules'. It may therefore come as something of a shock to the first-time reader of Statement 1.202 on Insolvency Practice to be confronted by a mass of what certainly look like regulations, couched in apparently legal phraseology and dealing with a score of specific situations.

In fact, this Statement – which was drawn up to confront the new insolvency roles created by the Insolvency Act 1986, but has been revised in detail twice since then – has been the subject of at least one attempt to rewrite it in more user-friendly language. However, at the end of the day, it is the *number* of insolvency roles and combinations of roles which have foiled CAJEC and the Ethics Committee of the Society of Practitioners of Insolvency (SPI), who have in effect joint responsibility for maintaining and updating this guidance, although it is, of course, the individual insolvency regulators who approve, publish and enforce it.

In an attempt to sort out the complexity of the possibilities, those responsible for the first draft Statement began by placing all the individual roles in a grid or matrix, so that their interaction on every other role could be plotted and agreed. Accordingly, it was decided that the same firm should not conduct an administration of a company following appointment as adminstrative or other receiver, should not follow appointment as administrative receiver by acceptance of appointment as supervisor of a voluntary arrangement, and so on. Other roles – for example, appointment as liquidator following acting as supervisor of a voluntary arrangement or as administrator – were acceptable in particular circumstances (or as the Framework might say, 'provided specified safeguards were in place').

It should be noted that the grid – and consequently the guidance which followed – dealt with *sequential* rather than *current* combinations. Where the latter are legally possible in relation to the same debtor they are likely to involve conflicts of interest – for example, the supervisor of a company voluntary arrangement (whose duty is presumably to the arrangement and its continuity) accepting simultaneous appointment as administrative receiver (where the duty is essentially to the debenture holder) – which may or may not be manageable.

That interaction between possibly conflicting roles occupies the middle section of the Statement. The first section consists of an introductory note counselling objectivity, guidance on avoiding obtaining insolvency work by unlawful means or by improper solicitation (cross-referenced to Statement 1.211 on Obtaining Professional Work), a paragraph (4.0) advising caution in accepting appointments not featured in the guidance and recommending the relevant helpline if in doubt, and a note (4.2) on joint appointments, which cannot cure a basic conflict with the guidance provisions.

The middle section also contains guidance of greatest practical significance, including the definition of 'a material professional relationship', which, if it had applied to a firm within the preceding three years, rules out the acceptance of virtually all insolvency roles – save for the 'insolvency role' that is not an insolvency role, appointment under a member's voluntary liquidation. (Although the last-mentioned is not an insolvency appointment in reality, it does of course require an insolvency *licence*.)

The final section of the Statement (paragraphs 17.0 to 23.1) deals with a number of miscellaneous situations and considerations, none of which have caused particular difficulty in interpretation or practice, save that paragraph 22.0 applies to 'relationship with a debenture holder' – and the considerations surrounding the relationship of an investigating accountant with the debenture holder who might ultimately appoint him or her as administrative receiver do feature in the financial press with monotonous (for the profession) regularity. Paragraph 23.0 constitutes a comprehensive warning against anyone in a firm acquiring assets of a debtor in respect of whom a member of the firm holds an insolvency appointment.

The mechanistic approach to the drafting of Statement 1.202 has two implications which are not, generally, shared with the rest of the Guide to Professional Ethics:

1 A member is generally entitled to assume that if the role he or she envisages accepting does not involve circumstances specifically proscribed by the Statement, and there are no particular threats to objectivity, he or she may go ahead and accept.

2 Although this is still *guidance* rather than *regulations*, it is guidance that it is

very hard to ignore. There have been few instances indeed where a member has acted against the letter of a Statement 1.202 provision and avoided an adverse disciplinary finding – despite the most expert legal assistance.

Reference to 'expert … assistance' could prompt the identification of a further distinction between Statement 1.202 and the rest of the Guide: those who are the subject of complaint for alleged failures to follow the Statement 1.202 guidance are very often the leaders of the insolvency branch of the profession. The typical defendant before the Disciplinary Committee is a sole or small practitioner for whom things have, in one way or another, become too much.

Because the Statement is framed in legalistic or literal terms, it to a large extent speaks for itself. The professional bodies receive quite a number of enquiries from large firms of insolvency practitioners, generally in respect of combinations of appointments to associates of the debtor or of the firm The advisory services consider each enquiry on its merits, resorting to the assistance of an insolvency specialist where necessary.

It is often helpful for advisers to check their conclusion by reference to the two main criteria applied by the original working party in relation to the 'grid':

1 Is the 'accountability' of the practitioner or his firm in any previous role properly preserved? For example, is there no real danger that he might have to sue himself or his partners? (What the Framework would call a self-review threat.)
2 Could the participation of the practitioner in the previous role create a conflict of interest, in particular by placing him too close to the debtor, its managers, or any other relevant party?

COMMON AREAS OF ENQUIRY

General, untutored enquiries about the guidance on insolvency practice are, for at least two reasons, not very common:

1 As we have already noted, the *tone* of the guidance of Statement 1.202 is very detailed and specific, and great effort has been expended to avoid ambiguity.
2 Those with a prime interest in this guidance are *specialists* – that is, the insolvency branch of the profession – and a detailed working knowledge of the Statement is a prerequisite to engaging in practice safely.

Most of the run-of-the-mill enquiries relate to six paragraphs in the middle section, those dealing with 'material professional relationships' (paragraphs 8.0–8.3) or the situation already identified as 'in the news' – appointment as investigating accountant in the light of a possible subsequent adminstrative receivership (8.4 – 8.5).

Material professional relationship

The main point to bear in mind is that this guidance (originally entitled 'Continuing professional relationship') has been the subject of progressive *broadening*, so that it should by now apply to all relevant relationships (paragraphs 8.0–8.3), that is:

● with a client or former client within the last three years;
● with a director or shadow director of a client or former client;
● with associates or subsidiaries of a client or former client, provided that the relationship is material in the context of the debtor;
● in respect of audit work, continuing work, or individual assignments 'of such overall significance or in such circumstances that a member's objectivity in carrying out a subsequent insolvency appointment could be or could reasonably be seen to be prejudiced'; or
● on behalf of a firm, a principal or employee of the firm, an associate firm or a firm with which a relevant individual has previously been associated.

As has previously been noted, a relationship which satisfies any of the permutations listed above will normally prevent acceptance of any insolvency appointment.

Appointment as investigating accountant (at the instigation of a creditor (paragraphs 8.4–8.5)

This much publicised situation arises where a firm (which probably has a longstanding connection with a particular bank or other finance house) is requested by the bank – but usually via the debtor company – to carry out an investigation into the financial health of the company. The individual or firm appointed to investigate will know from previous experience that if he or she recommends that the debenture holder initiates administrative receivership, then he or she or the firm are overwhelmingly likely to receive a subsequent appointment.

The threats to objectivity which are generally identified in the press are twofold:

1 A 'carrot' threat in respect of obtaining the subsequent receivership.
2 A conflict between the interests of the company and its management (which presumably would like to go on trading, even if no profitability corner is

likely to be turned) and those of the debenture holder (which is primarily concerned in protecting its investment).

These alleged problems for the investigating accountant and his or her objectivity are, in the view of the insolvency profession, more speculative than real. So far as the 'carrot' threat is concerned, this is not just a feature of investigating accountants. It arises in relation to virtually every professional role, from the surgeon who has to decide whether or not to recommend an operation, which the surgeon will inevitably carry out, to the barrister who advises his or her client on whether or not to appeal against a court's decision, knowing that he or she will be handling the appeal.

So far as the conflict of interest is concerned, this does not involve the investigating accountant *provided that*, in the words of paragraph 8.4 (b): 'the practice has its principal client relationship with the creditor or other party, rather than with the company or proprietor of the business, and the company or the proprietor of the business is aware of this.' Nevertheless there is anecdotal evidence – mainly from the disappointed management of bankrupted companies – that investigating accountants have from time to time made the wrong recommendation. To date virtually none of this evidence has resulted in either a successful legal action or disciplinary measures against the accountant. On the other hand, statistics are quoted in the profession which would indicate that investigating accountants are not at all keen to comment adversely, and that receivership only follows investigation in a minority of cases. Practitioners maintain that if they were to report unduly unfavourably in any number of cases, the debenture holders would quickly dispense with their services.

At the end of the day it is of course the attitude of the debenture holder that is decisive. However, firms may make life unduly difficult for themselves – to the point of attracting unfavourable press comment – by offering to carry out investigations at a cut price, or for nothing, or – even worse – on some sort of contingent basis.

A FUTURE WITH THE FRAMEWORK?

We have already noted the pledge of CAJEC and the Institutes to take a fresh look at the whole of the Guide from the point of view of Framework applicability. Statement 1.202, with its two immediate successors, may therefore be in the front line for such consideration, which, on the basis of past practice, would be conducted jointly with the Ethics Committee of the Society of Practitioners of Insolvency (SPI). In further accordance with established practice, any such review would only be carried out after extensive consultation.

It is not the place of this volume to examine the arguments for and against such a course. It is perhaps, however, worth mentioning that the concept of 'managing conflict' was first raised in relation to the new (1986) guidance on insolvency practice. Ethical archaeologists should pitch their tents around paragraph 18.0 – Other potential conflicts of interests:

(i) Group, Associated and family-connected companies:
Members should be particularly aware of the difficulties likely to arise from the existence of inter-company transactions or guarantees in group, associated or 'family-connected' company situations. Acceptance of an insolvency appointment in relation to more than one company in the group or association may raise issues of conflict of interest. Nevertheless it may be impracticable for a series of different insolvency practitioners to act. A member should not accept multiple appointments in such situations *unless he is satisfied that he is able to take steps to minimise problems of conflict and that his overall integrity and objectivity are, and are seen to be, maintained.* (emphasis added)

So here we have, in an embryo form, an excellent example of:

1 the identification of a threat;
2 the requirement to implement safeguards; and
3 a final requirement that overall integrity and objectivity may be demonstrated to be maintained.

The safeguards are not, it will be observed, detailed. One recognised safeguard (or step to minimise the problems of conflict) is for the appointee to instruct different firms of solicitors in relation to each of the debtors, and be seen to act on the basis of their advice.

Relevant Queries

Q   *'Material' occurs several times in paragraphs 8.0 to 8.2. Is help given anywhere as to the interpretation of 'material'?*

A   Not as such. However, the guidance does place the word in context more than once, for example:
(a)   audit work is invariably material (8.0(i));
(b)   'assignments' become material when they are of 'such overall significance or in such circumstances' that objectivity could reasonably be seen to be prejudiced (8.0(ii));
(c)   materiality in relationship to work for associates of the debtor is materiality in relation to the *debtor* him or itself (8.1).

CHAPTER 9

Corporate finance advice

The Statement on Corporate Finance Advice of the UK and Irish Accountancy bodies is unique in a number of ways:

- It has no equivalent in either the IFAC Code, or the ethical guidance of most other national bodies.
- It is directed 'to all members', and not just those in practice or business.
- It contains a Guidance Note by way of annex, on 'Compliance with the City Code on Takeovers and Mergers' incorporated at the specific request of the City Panel, which deals with the responsibilities of members providing takeover services *so far as the Panel, rather than the Institutes are concerned.*

This last-mentioned was included, after considerable soul-searching, in the second edition of the Statement, issued in 1992. The Statement was first issued on 1 September 1989, and the present, third edition dates from 1 April 1995. There is an asterisked note on the first page of the current Statement, indicating that CAJEC is consulting on due diligence assignments, and the extent to which they are compatible with reporting roles. The result is likely to be the issue of a further (fourth) version of the Statement, within a timescale of only seven years. This frequency of review represents not so much fussiness on the part of the bodies as an acceptance that once detailed guidance on a specialist area involving clear public interest considerations is issued, there is a responsibility to keep it up to date. (Much the same could be said about the preceding Statement on Insolvency Practice.)

The Statement was first conceived in response to a request from the Panel for the bodies to look at the situation of a firm of auditors which found itself acting for both sides in a contested takeover. This occupies the first and major part of the Statement itself, after the introductory note and references to the Takeover Panel and the Stock Exchange.

This first section illustrates well the practical need for guidance measures which can enable an accountancy firm to continue to act for more than one client, even though circumstances may have brought the interests of those clients into conflict. If the concept of management of conflict was first publicly aired in the Statement on Insolvency Practice (1.202) in relation to the potential conflicts of interest arising out of 'group, associated and family-connected companies' (see previous chapter), it received its significant development in this guidance on corporate finance advice. Indeed, as we shall see, the list of safeguards required in connection with management of conflict situations which appears at paragraph 6.0 of Statement 1.203, is repeated word for word in the following Statement on 'Conflicts of Interest'(1.204). It is probably appropriate to set them out at this stage:

a. **the use of different partners and teams for different engagements;**
b. **all necessary steps to prevent leakage of confidential information between different teams and sections within the firm;**
c. **regular review of the situation by a senior partner or compliance officer not personally involved with either client; and**
d. **advising the clients to seek additional independent advice.**

These safeguards are of course very much in accordance with those referred to in the Framework (see Chapter 7), and no doubt contributed to the subsequent development of the Framework concept.

The corporate finance guidance is postulated on the basis that for an audit firm to cease to act for either party in a contested takeover, and therefore deprive them, the market and the public of the availability of up-to-date financial information just when it is likely to be needed, is in no one's interest. 'Accordingly in such circumstances a firm may continue to act for more than one party as auditor, as reporting accountants on any profit forecast, and in the provision of incidental advice consistent with these roles' (paragraph 4.2). There must, however, be limitations on the firm's provision of other, possibly executive functions, and these differ according to whether the takeover transaction is subject to the City Code (paragraph 4.2) or whether it is not (paragraph 4.5).

Where the takeover is subject to the City Code: 'the firm should not act as lead adviser for any party involved or issue a critique of a client's accounts and should implement proper safeguards'. The 'safeguards' are those set out above, and 'lead adviser' is defined as 'the firm or person primarily responsible for advising on, organising and presenting an offer or the response to an offer'.

Where the takeover is not subject to the Code 'and there is no substantial public interest involved' a firm may advise either or *both* sides, again subject to the implementation of appropriate safeguards. The firm has to have regard to the interests of minority shareholders, and from the point of view of ensuring their protection 'should consider the desirability of one company having a wholly independent adviser'.

This guidance has caused remarkably little difficulty in operation, which may indicate that the accountancy bodies have 'pitched it about right'. Nevertheless, at the time of the issue of the guidance in 1989 there was considerable controversy, with professional interests displaying anxiety – in particular about the 'lead adviser' restriction in relation to takeovers subject to the Code – while established corporate finance organisations were apparently aggrieved that accountants were able to enter upon their preserves at all!

Subsequent sections of the Statement have aroused less controversy. The first deals with promoting an issue or sale, and firms are adjured (paragraph 4.6) not to 'underwrite or promote an issue or sale to the public of shares or securities of the company on which (the firm) has reported or is to report ... involvement of this kind would endanger the independence of the firm in the audit and/or reporting function'. This is very much on all fours with paragraph 4.72 of Statement 1.201 ('Other services' – see Chapter 7).

There follows a more general section on 'avoiding conflicts of interest', which features the safeguards quoted above, and counsels, in addition, that:

> **All reasonable steps should be taken to ascertain whether a conflict of interest exists or is likely to arise in the future between a firm and its clients, both in regard to new engagements and to the changing circumstances of existing clients, and including any implications arising from the possession of confidential information.**

A review of such relationships is recommended 'before accepting a new appointment and regularly thereafter'.

This paragraph (5.0) also contains what amounts to a (discretionary) quarantine period: 'A relationship which ended over two years before is unlikely to constitute a conflict.' That two-year period is consistent with the 'two years of clear water under the bridge' before a former officer or employee of a company should participate in the audit of that company. It should, however, be contrasted with the *five*-year quarantine period which follows mandatory rotation of an audit engagement partner (see Chapter 7), and the *three*-year *cordon sanitaire* which applies in insolvency cases.

Appropriate disclosure is a requirement (or further safeguard) where a non-material conflict of interests arises. This should normally be in writing, and if such disclosure 'would seriously prejudice the interests of a client', the firm should not be the lead adviser for two or more clients (paragraphs 5.2–5.3).

The next section in this comprehensive (or heterogeneous, according to your view) Statement represents an addition introduced in the current version of the guidance, following the London Stock Exchange's introduction of a new potential role for firms of accountants, that of *sponsor*. In fact we have already considered guidance which reflects the LSE's introduction of sponsorship – rephrasing of paragraph 4.6 so as to remove the former prohibition on sponsorship, at any event to the extent permitted in the LSE Yellow Book, which lists tasks, essentially of a compliance, advisory or reporting nature, or that do not on the face of it conflict with acting as auditor. (In addition a warning has been introduced in paragraph 1.0, Introductory Note, against 'corporate finance activities such as promoting, marketing or placing securities (which) contain so strong an element of advocacy as to be incompatible with the objectivity required ... of an auditor or reporting accountant'.)

The two final sections of the Statement deal with 'documents for client and public use' and 'fees'. The latter is little more than a cross-reference to Statement 1.210 (see Chapter 16). However the section (paragraphs 7.0–7.6) on 'documents' is useful, and indeed of potentially wider application. For example:

> **Any statements or observations in a document prepared for a client must be such as, taken individually and as a whole, are justifiable on an objective examination of the available facts. (7.1)**
> **In the case of a document prepared solely for the client and its professional advisers, it should be a condition of the engagement that the document should not be disclosed to any third party without the firm's express permission. (7.2)**
> **A firm must take responsibility for anything published under its name, and the published document should make clear the client for whom the firm is acting. (7.5)**

The guidance also becomes specific in matters which might be considered to border on the technical – see in particular paragraphs 7.4 (assumptions) and 7.6 (disclosure of roles of various advisers).

This chapter opened with a reference to the Guidance Note requiring compliance with the City Code. In addition to general compliance with the Code, the Note includes a 'cold-shouldering' requirement (paragraph 3.1).

Neither the Statement itself, nor the Annex (Guidance Note) have, it has been noted, created significant problems in practice. It was pointed out at the beginning of this chapter that the Statement is also of application to all members. Inevitably, issues of corporate finance will arise from time to time among the enquiries dealt with by, for example, the ICAEW's IMACE service (for members in business). These are very likely to involve price-sensitive information – and this is one of the reasons why IMACE procedures are founded on absolute confidentiality.

Notes

1 **In late 1995 CAJEC consulted ('White Paper') on new guidance on due diligence work and contingent fees. This is likely to be reflected in changes to Statement 1.203 during the course of 1996.**

2 The ACCA Rules (qv) do not contain all the provisions indicated in this chapter, in particular the latest additions of guidance on LSE 'sponsorship', or the Annex relating to the City Code. However, a requirement to observe the Code is included in the Rules.

CHAPTER 10

Conflicts of interest

A separate Statement on conflicts of interest dates from the issue of the substantially revised Guide to Professional Ethics in February 1992. Before that, elements of the present guidance were to be found in the existing independence guidance and, from 1989, in the guidance reviewed in the previous chapter on corporate finance advice. The (shortish) Statement first issued in 1992 contrasts the action to be taken by firms when their interests conflict with those of a client (paragraphs 2.0–2.1) with the situation when it is the interests of different clients which are in conflict (5.0–5.5).

CONFLICT BETWEEN A FIRM'S INTERESTS AND THOSE OF ITS CLIENT

The guidance here is really very simple: a firm should withdraw from or refuse to act in any engagement where there is likely to be a significant conflict of interests between itself and the client. Paragraph 2.1 states that: 'any material financial gain which … is likely to accrue to the firm as a result of the engagement (otherwise than in the form of fees or other reward from the client for its services or commission, etc. properly earned) … will *always* amount to a significant conflict of interest.' (emphasis added)

CONFLICT BETWEEN INTERESTS OF DIFFERENT CLIENTS

Here, as we have seen in connection with corporate finance advice, the situation is rather different:

> **There is, on the face of it, nothing improper in a firm having two or more clients whose interests may be in conflict. In such a case, however, the work of the firm should be so managed as to avoid the interests of one client adversely affecting those of another. (5.0)**

The detailed guidance which follows this proposition does indeed bear a close resemblance to the relevant section of the Statement on corporate finance advice, the core guidance on 'safeguards' being identical. Here too *disclosure* is featured as a necessary preliminary to the management of any conflict.

Interestingly, sole practitioners and small firms are singled out for attention (5.4) without the inclusion of any 'exemption' comparable with that relating to, for example, trustee shareholdings (see Chapter 6). The guidance eventually recognises that the freedom of action of a sole practitioner or firm will be limited by the fact that three out of four of the listed safeguards (different teams, compartmentalisation, and review by a senior partner or compliance officer) are not likely to be available. The decision of the practitioner or firm 'should take account of (this) fact'.

The current guidance does not include any specific examples of conflict situations, whereas at least two were featured in the pre-1992 guidance. One of those situations still features quite regularly among the enquiries received by the Institute helplines, and is considered in the queries section at the end of this chapter.

COMMISSION

Guidance on 'commission, fee, reward or other benefit' received from a third party as a consequence of advising a client to pursue a particular course of conduct is the middle section of Statement 1.204. This guidance has recently been extended, in line with guidance published within the last few years by the Law Society. This reflects not only the consideration that the retention of commission is essentially a *legal* issue, but also that the former guidance of both bodies has been diagnosed as not representing the legal position sufficiently comprehensively.

The new element in the guidance of the accountancy bodies is the emphasis on the duty to *account for commission* to the client. This not only requires the *notification* to the client of the fact that commission will be received, and of the amount of such commission (as soon as that is known), but also that the professional adviser, whether he or she be acting as *agent* or in what is called a *fiduciary* capacity, is bound to pay the commission, fee, reward, and so forth, over to the client unless he or she has secured the latter's permission to retain it.

The new guidance is designed to dovetail with more detailed requirements relating to investment business commissions. The guidance of Statement 1.204 is necessarily succinct, and useful extra information may be gleaned from a study of the relevant Investment Business Regulations issued by the bodies.

In the case of ICAEW, further explanation is also given in Section 1.314 of the Members' Handbook, issued at the same time as the extended ethical guidance and investment business regulations. In particular, Section 1.314

summarises in a convenient form the 'Options' in relation to retention of commission. (The guidance of ACCA does not, as yet, contain this new element of 'accounting for commission', but ACCA members are, of course, subject to the same legal duties as others acting in a fiduciary capacity.)

If the accountant is *not* acting as the client's agent or in a fiduciary capacity, then the duty to account for commission and so on may be waived. One likely circumstance where the duty would not arise is where the office of a firm is also a building society agency, and clients do business with the agency – for instance, depositing savings – without any specific reference to the principals or staff of the firm. Such circumstances are, however, very specific and limited, and practising accountants should be reluctant to assume that they are relieved of the duty, unless they have had that confirmed by their solicitors.

Relevant Queries

Q1 *I am aware that a client company has premises on the market which would be very suitable for our firm. There is no 'For Sale' sign on the premises, and they have not as yet been advertised. Would it represent a conflict of interest if I were to make an offer for the premises, either directly, or anonymously through a third party?*

A1 The effect of both Statement 1.204 on conflicts of interest and the following Statement, 1.205 on *confidentiality*, would be that you should not take advantage of an existing client for your own gain. However, it would be unreasonable for your client to be deprived of the possibility of an acceptable offer, just because it comes from your firm. You could not be subject to criticism if you were (a) to indicate your interest to the client, and (b) to recommend him to seek independent professional advice. It is implicit in the above that an 'anonymous' offer would be open to the worst construction.

Q2 *Our firm has previously acted for a company run by a husband and wife, and for each of them in relation to their personal affairs. The couple are now in the process of divorce. Can we properly continue to act for either or both of the parties? We should prefer to continue to act for the husband, because the wife has now withdrawn from the company and we do not wish to lose its audit.*

A2 Some advice on similar situations appeared in the pre-1992 guidance, which indicated that you should consider seriously whether you are able to act for both, or even one of the parties. In such situations, if you express a desire to continue to act for one of the parties, say, the husband – the other party is likely to withdraw their instructions, coupled quite often with a contention by their solicitors that you should cease to act for either.

Having regard to the guidance on management of conflict situations, a decision by your firm to cease to act for *one* of the parties should normally be sustainable, on the assumption that you are able to implement the safeguards referred to in paragraph 5.3 of Statement 1.204.

CHAPTER 11

Confidentiality

This Statement (1.205) contains long-standing guidance, and applies 'to all members'. It is divided into two sections, the first relating to improper *disclosure* of information acquired in the course of professional work, and the second to improper *use* of such information.

It is a cardinal principle of work in any profession that information acquired in relation to the affairs of a client should be treated with the utmost confidentiality. This is no doubt part of the 'fiduciary duty' which applies to most professional situations, and its basis is accordingly essentially legal.

The duty of an employee, whether he be a professional person or not, is the subject of a separate strand of legal case law. However, the considerations are, for practical purposes, sufficiently close to allow for incorporation of them both in the same guidance.

Further (separate) guidance on disclosure is given to ICAEW members in the Section 1.306 for members in practice (Section 1.308 gives advice on disclosure in taxation matters) and Section 1.402 for members in business. (Section 1.306 has been subject to recent extensive revision and the tax elements were reissued in November 1995 as 'Tax 27/95' – now incorporated in Section 1.308.) Members in doubt as to their position are advised to consult their solicitor or the relevant Institute helplines (paragraph 1.2, Statement 1.205).

DISCLOSURE – EXEMPTIONS

Paragraph 1.0 of the Statement advises that:

> **Information confidential to a client or employer acquired in the course of professional work should not be disclosed except where consent has been obtained from the client, employer or other proper source, or where there is a legal right or duty to disclose.**

As has been indicated, Sections 1.306 and 1.402 of the ICAEW Handbook do give more detailed advice on the essentially legal elements of disclosure. It may, however, be helpful here to summarise the recognised exceptions to the duty of professional confidentiality, that is, those situations where the professional adviser (or employee) may properly disclose otherwise confidential information. The clue is given by the words 'a legal right or duty to disclose'.

One should note first of all that disclosure may be made where the client or employer consents to such disclosure. Difficulties occasionally arise in the case of companies which have gone into liquidation. In such cases, it is the liquidator who may give the relevant consent.

To return to the 'legal right or duty to disclose', the first refers to:

1 the legal right to disclose confidential information where one's own interests require it; and
2 disclosure where that is justified in the public interest.

(These are technical areas on which helpful advice is given in Section A of 1.306 and Part 2 of Section 1.402 of the ICAEW Handbook, and equivalent guidance of the other bodies.)

'A legal ... duty to disclose' arises as a result of relevant statutory provisions, of which the best examples are such areas as treason, terrorist offences in Northern Ireland and money laundering. Since paragraph 1.0 was first formulated, however, a further *professional* duty to disclose has been developing so far as the auditor is concerned. This relates essentially to disclosure to *regulators*, in respect of the activities of clients in regulated areas. Reference should be made, where appropriate, to Statement of Auditing Standards 620 and to relevant Auditing Guidelines and Practice Notes.

IMPROPER USE OF INFORMATION

Paragraph 2.0 sets out the principle:

A member acquiring or receiving confidential information in the course of his or her professional work should neither use nor appear to use that information for his or her personal advantage or for the advantage of a third party.

There is clearly an overlap here with the guidance in the previous Statement on conflicts between the interests of the firm and those of clients. Using confidential information belonging to a client for one's own purposes would clearly contravene the provisions of paragraphs 2.0 and 2.1 of Statement 1.204. However, in those paragraphs, ceasing to act for the client may be a possible way out of the impasse, whereas it would still be quite wrong for a firm to make improper use of confidential information even in respect of a client for whom they had ceased to act.

There is a similar duty in relation to confidential information gained during employment. An employee is expected to maintain *loyalty* towards an existing employer. It is, however, in my understanding, open to some doubt as to how far the duty of loyalty might extend following cessation of employment – at any event in relation to a *professional* employee. CAJEC is, at the time of writing, considering new user-friendly guidance for members in business, and it may be that when (or if) this is adopted by the bodies, it may shed more light on what is a difficult area, both legally and ethically. It may not be entirely accidental that the detailed 'discussion' in paragraph 2.0 of Statement 1.205 relates rather more to employment than it does to practice issues.

Relevant Queries

Q1   *I am owed fees by a client company, which has just been placed in (creditors' voluntary) liquidation. I believe that the conduct of the directors of the company, during its last months of trading, may not have been entirely honest and scrupulous. I am intending to go to the creditors' meeting. How much information about the company's affairs can I properly disclose?*

A1   You do have the right to disclose confidential information where that is required in your own interests. There is relevant guidance on this area in paragraph 18 of Section 1.306 in the ICAEW Members' Handbook. It includes as a circumstance, 'to enable the member to sue for his fees'.

That exemption, of course, only relates to such disclosure as is *reasonably necessary* to enable the member to sue. It does not give the member *carte blanche* to defame the directors at a creditors' meeting.

If you do have something more than mere suspicion that the directors may, for example, be guilty of fraudulent or wrongful trading, then you might be free to disclose relevant information – but you would have to be prepared to defend any disclosure on the basis that it was justified in the public interest.

If a liquidator had been appointed, you could seek his consent to disclose, since he then constitutes the management of the company.

CHAPTER 12

Changes in a professional appointment

The guidance on this subject goes back a very long way, predating the Guide to Professional Ethics. In January 1995 the existing guidance was amalgamated, and is now all contained in Statement 1.206.

PROCEDURE OF PROFESSIONAL ENQUIRY

The Statement sets out a procedure of professional enquiry between a prospective new appointee and the existing appointment-holder. The reason for such communication is set out in the discussion section which follows the initial summary (paragraph 1.0). Interestingly, the first principle stated in that paragraph is that: 'clients have the right to choose their auditors and other professional advisers, and to change to others if they so desire.' That is clearly a principle which goes beyond the guidance on change in appointment.

Paragraph 1.3 sets out the justification for this procedure – which may sound very strange to lawyers in particular – in the following terms:

The purpose of finding out the background to the proposed change is to enable the member to determine whether, in all circumstances, it would be proper for him or her to accept the assignment. In particular, members nominated as auditors will wish to ensure that they do not unwittingly become the means by which any unsatisfactory practices of the company or any impropriety in the conduct of its affairs may be enabled to continue or may be concealed from shareholders or other legitimately interested persons. Communication is meant to ensure that all relevant facts are known to the member who, having considered them, is then entitled to accept the nomination if he wishes so to do.

The effect is that, for many, many years, the accountancy profession has identified the principal public interest arising from change in a professional appointment as being that the new adviser should be *warned* about the circumstances in which his or her predecessor has ceased to act. A dishonest client cannot rely on sacking the incumbent and then being able to go behind his or her back to instruct a potentially more complaisant successor who is substantially ignorant of the client's infamy! At a somewhat less sensational level, the procedure means that a potential replacement should be sufficiently 'briefed' about any dispute in relation to accounting treatments which is likely to re-emerge to haunt him.

The current guidance is very recent, and designed to be user-friendly. Accordingly it is probably unnecessary to repeat in detail the procedure indicated in paragraphs 1.4–1.11. Points for possible comment include the following:

1 The initial duty to make contact lies with the proposed successor (1.4).
2 The proposed successor 'should ask the client to inform the existing auditor or adviser of the proposed change and, at the same time, to give the latter written authority to discuss the client's affairs with the member' (1.5). If that authority is not forthcoming, the guidance provides that 'the existing auditor or adviser should report that fact to the prospective auditor or adviser who should not accept nomination/appointment' (1.7).

   This might imply that the permission of the client is a *legal* requirement to enable the existing adviser to disclose confidential issues. However, a moment's thought will indicate that this is not the case. The consent of the client is hardly likely to be *consent to defame him at will*! It is therefore probable that the purpose of this provision, requiring the potential successor to decline to act, is to protect the latter from having to exercise his or her discretion in difficult circumstances, and having to justify such an exercise to the client. Far simpler to say, 'you must not act'.
3 The guidance indicates that it is 'not sufficient [for the existing adviser] to state [in his or her reply to the enquiry] that unspecified factors exist'. He or she must be prepared to specify those factors within his or her knowledge of which a successor should properly be aware.

   What if that knowledge is more in the nature of unsubstantiated suspicion than actual evidence? The guidance provides in such circumstances that if the incumbent prefers to explain the factors orally, his or her prospective successor should be prepared to confer, 'and each should make their own record of such a discussion' (1.8).
4 If the existing adviser does not respond within a reasonable time, the prospective successor has two courses of action open to him or her:
   (a) report the other member to his or her Investigation Committee, and/or
   (b) adopt the procedure indicated in paragraph 1.10 – trying to get in touch by other means, concluding with a final letter by recorded delivery service 'stating that unless he receives a reply within a specified time he will assume that there are no matters … that should be brought to his attention'.

5 The procedure applies whether or not the advisers concerned are members of a relevant professional body. However if the incumbent is a non-member it will (probably) be impossible to compel him or her to reply, and the procedure of paragraph 1.10 may have to be invoked. (There is no objection to the proposed appointee 'leap- frogging' a predecessor who refuses to reply, and consulting *his or her* predecessor – although any information held by the latter may well be historic.)

COMMUNICATION

Under this subheading, paragraph 1.15 indicates a number of relevant 'factors' that should be communicated.

UNPAID FEES

We should first of all record that this is an area in which the guidance of ACCA differs from that of the three Institutes. For some time, the Chartered Association has required the provision of minimal handover information even if fees are outstanding. This is potentially very helpful in breaking the 'log jam' which can exist where the incumbent is owed money but is not prepared to sue for his or her fees. (It may well be uneconomic to do so, where the amount at issue is only a few hundred pounds.)

That provision does not, for better or for worse, have any equivalent in the guidance of the Institutes, despite proposals to that effect to their Councils. (It has been rumoured that ACCA are reconsidering their position on the issue, so as to bring it into line with the three Institutes.)

The situation so far as the Institutes are concerned is set out, in fact, in a later Statement 1.210, on Fees, at paragraph 3.2:

> **A member whose fees have not been paid may be entitled to retain certain books and papers of a client upon which he has been working by exercising a lien and may refuse to pass on information to the client or his successor accountant until those fees are paid. However a member who so acts should be prepared to take reasonable steps to resolve any dispute relating to the amount of that fee.**

Thus paragraph 3.0 of 1.206, headed 'Co-operation with a successor' is often frustrated, at any event so far as the provision of 'information as to the client's affairs, lack of which might prejudice the client's interests' is confirmed. The second element – that no charge should be made for such handover information

– is enforceable, unless the incumbent is able to argue that there is a 'significant amount of work involved'. The relevant ethics committees have equated 'significant' with 'unusual'. It follows that the imposition of a standard charge for handover information is against both the spirit and the letter of the guidance.

TRANSFER OF BOOKS AND PAPERS

The effect of the paragraph just quoted from Statement 1.210 is also, of course, that the requirement for prompt transfer of a client's papers to the successor, after the latter has been duly appointed, may also be frustrated – in this case, by the incumbent exercising a lien. There are, however, a number of limitations on the exercise of lien – for example, the statutory books and accounting records of an incorporated company are not subject to such a lien – and helpful advice is given in ICAEW Section 1.302 and equivalent guidance of the other bodies.

ADDITIONAL WORK

The full requirement for 'professional enquiry' only exists where work currently being carried on by one accountant is to cease, and be taken over by the proposed successor. Where work additional to that currently being carried on is proposed, the duty on the new appointee is only to 'notify (the) other professional adviser of the work he has been asked to undertake' (4.0).

The discussion paragraphs which follow explain the reasoning behind this requirement – mainly clarification of the position between the advisers, coupled with the possibility of the existing adviser providing relevant information to the new appointee – together with the advice that notification need not be given if 'the client advances reasons which persuade the firm that, in all the circumstances, the existing adviser should not be informed' (4.2). The secretariat is sometimes asked to pronounce on the validity of quite specious 'reasons', including the fact that the client owes money to the existing adviser. Something more than this is clearly needed. In any event, members who do reach such a conclusion would be well advised to document both the client's request and reasons, and the considerations which the firm found convincing.

Relevant Queries

Q *I've asked A.B. & Co. for professional clearance in relation to a change of appointment, and they are refusing to reply because they say they are owed money. (This enquiry is recorded not because of any merit, but because it is* *probably the single most frequent enquiry received by the secretariats of the bodies!)*

A First, you should be aware that there is no such thing as 'professional clearance' – in the sense of any sort of permission which the existing adviser can give to, or withhold from his or her successor. The procedure is rather one of professional enquiry (see above).

A.B. & Co. cannot refuse to answer your professional enquiry on the grounds that fees are outstanding, since their duty to respond is 'absolute' (see paragraph 1.8). Further, 'the existence of unpaid fees is not of itself a reason' why a prospective auditor or adviser should not accept nomination/appointment (paragraph 1.17). He may, if he wishes, use his good offices to assist in settlement of the fee, but he is under no obligation to do so.

However, A.B. & Co. may be acting in accordance with the guidance of the three UK & Irish Institutes, in withholding handover information (see paragraph 3.2, Statement 1.210). If, though, they are ACCA members, they are bound by the guidance of their own body to co-operate, at any event in relation to minimal information.

CHAPTER 13

Consultancy

This is a very short Statement (1.207), which it is practical to quote in full:

This Statement applies only to practising members, affiliates and, where appropriate, employees of practising firms.

1.0 If a member in practice (the practitioner) obtains the advice of a member (the consultant) on a consultancy basis on behalf of a client, the consultant or any practising firm with which he or his consultancy organisation is associated should not, without the consent of the practitioner, accept from that client within three years of completion of the consultancy assignment, any work which was, at the time the consultant was first retained in relation to that client's affairs, being carried out by the practitioner.

2.0 The same considerations apply where a practitioner introduces one of his clients to the consultant for the purposes of consultancy.

NOT A RESTRICTIVE PRACTICE!

At first sight this restriction upon the 'consultant' firm's accepting instructions from the referred client for three years from completion of the consultancy assignment looks like a very blatant example of restrictive trade practices, sustaining the existing adviser, and preventing the newcomer (at any event so far as the client is concerned) from gaining work. However the original purpose of this guidance (which was one of the Statements in the first Guide to Professional Ethics), was to *encourage* work – that is to say, consultancy work – rather than inhibit it.

The age of the Statement is important. It dates from a period when the major firms were beginning to expand into a range of consultancy activities, while smaller firms were effectively restricted to audit and taxation work. Those smaller firms had, accordingly, a quite natural fear that if their clients became familiar with the additional breadth of service provided by larger firms, they would be lost. The purpose of the guidance was therefore to provide reassurance to the smaller practitioner that he or she could refer a client to a larger firm, for specialist consultancy services, without imperilling his or her continuing to act for the client in respect of non-consultancy services.

The inability of a small firm to provide consultancy services in-house is still a feature of the current accountancy scene. Accordingly, successive ethics committees considering the merits of 1.207 have concluded that it is 'safer to leave it in place for the time being'. The committees have, indeed, sometimes been inclined to stretch the application of the guidance to referred work that is not specifically consultancy.

From time to time, however, practitioners will seek to apply this guidance so as to restrict *subcontractors* from accepting instructions from clients of the practitioner. In such cases, the committees have tended to rely on a timeworn precedent of the 'old' ICAEW Ethics Committee, which advised that subcontractors were not debarred from accepting instructions from clients of the person to whom they subcontracted their services provided that:

1 there was no improper solicitation; and
2 the practitioner had not protected his or her position by obtaining a legal commitment from the subcontractor that the latter would not accept such clients.

CHAPTER 14

Agencies

Statement 1.208 on Agencies was drafted in the aftermath of the Financial Services Act 1986, which we have referred to earlier as being the first measure in the new wave of 'self-regulation' by the professions. The Statement was designed to 'mop up' miscellaneous guidance considerations which were not strictly within the Investment Business Regulations of the Institutes. Accordingly the Statement contains a miscellany of guidance, following an introductory note which does little more than refer members in authorised firms to the Investment Business Regulations.

The Statement goes on to consider associations, expressly with building societies, where a firm may find itself in difficulty, either because it becomes an 'appointed representative' (more familiarly, tied agent) – an option which is not open to practising members – or because the society with whom it has relations is itself an appointed representative.

The theme behind the various provisions of 1.208 is *the preservation of 'professional independence'*. However, that 'independence' is very much in relation to the need to maintain an objective approach to investment advice, whether that should fall technically within the 1986 Act or not.

With its emphasis on the dangers of 'agency signs and literature', and conducting 'practices from premises which give the appearance of being a building society office', the statement has acquired something of a period 'air'. It is no secret that 1.208 is on CAJEC's 'shopping list' for review in the middle term. For the time being, members who are involved with building society agencies should consult the Statement with care, before embarking on any changes in their arrangements. One topic of regular enquiry in this area is featured in the example which follows.

Relevant Query

Q *The Joint Monitoring Unit has asked me to consult the Institute about the fascia of my office which, they say, gives the overall impression of a building society office, rather than an accountancy practice.*

A Avoiding the appearance of being a building society office is, of course, a requirement of paragraph 5.2 of Statement 1.208. This is a matter of consideration in relation to each particular set of office arrangements – the scope for variation of which is infinite. Arrangements which have led to criticism in the past include the following:

- A 'banner' building society sign which encompasses the whole width of the premises.
- Inadequate internal separation between the building society function – which should be at least a separate desk – and the practice reception.
- Building society literature 'straying' all over the ground floor (common) reception area, rather than being confined to the agency desk or counter.
- Inadequate directions in the common reception area to indicate where the offices of the accountancy firm are located.

CHAPTER 15

Associations with non-members

This was one of the Statements introduced in the revised 1992 Guide to Professional Ethics. Accordingly, it is framed in a way designed to be user-friendly, in that each of the main topics covered by the Statement is preceded by a clear heading.

It may be helpful for the reader to bear in mind that this guidance starts with 'mixed accountancy practices' (paragraph 1.0), and then works its way progressively outwards, via 'office-sharing' and other potentially confusing arrangements (paragraphs 2.0 – 2.2), to referral of work by non-member organisations. The whole tenor of the Statement (1.209) is to seek to ensure that arrangements between members and non-members are conducted in an ethical way, even though the matter may not be subject to the jurisdiction of any recognised professional body.

MIXED ACCOUNTANCY PRACTICES

Accordingly the guidance provides (1.0) that members who enter into practice with non-members are answerable to their professional body for the conduct of the latter. This is the case whether or not the non-members are affiliates of the professional body. (For more information on *affiliates*, see Chapter 21.)

The secretariats of the bodies are sometimes asked about the position of members who are consultants to non-member firms, or have a non-member consultant (for instance, a tax specialist) for their own firm. Such situations are clearly less than a mixed accountancy *practice*, and it is not therefore possible to rely on that guidance so as to hold a member responsible for the behaviour of the non-member consultant, or the non-member 'associate' shown on the member firm's letterheading. Nevertheless the Investigations Committees of the bodies do not regard themselves as powerless to deal with situations where the non-member non-partner is behaving in a way which is clearly at odds with the Guide to Professional Ethics.

Some assistance is given, as we shall see, in the third section of this

Statement. However, the committees have, on occasion, invoked the threat of disciplinary proceedings for the members concerned, inviting the latter to sever the connection with the offending non-member on pain of reference to the Disciplinary Committee. The foundation for such action is that a member who associates professionally with those whose conduct does not accord with the requirements of his or her professional body is bringing the profession into disrepute.

USE OF OFFICES AND NAMES

The principal object here (2.0–2.2) is to avoid confusion between a member firm, subject to professional standards and requirements, and an independent non-member organisation which is not so subject. Circumstances – including the financial constraints on 'young' practices – sometimes make it necessary for firms of professional accountants to operate under the same roof as accountants or others who are not professionally qualified. This may amount to 'office-sharing' between independent firms, or the core professional practice may have satellites or associates which are to a greater or lesser extent under its control.

In either case, the professional firm should exercise appropriate safeguards to ensure that the public are not misled as to the nature of the organisation with which they are dealing. (Similar considerations were indicated in the last chapter in relation to a practice 'sharing' with a building society agency.) The professional and non-professional entities should not use the same office, or the same telephone number, unless measures have been taken to make the distinction between them quite clear.

LENDING ONE'S QUALIFICATION

This section of the guidance goes on (2.2) to emphasise that a member should not allow a non-member to 'borrow' the member's firm's name, or his qualification (chartered or certified accountant) or the designatory letters associated with the qualification. The unprofessional nature of such a course is obvious, and the sanctions which the Investigation Committees can impose are those referred to earlier – principally threat of disciplinary proceedings in relation to conduct likely to bring the profession (or the member) into disrepute.

WORK FOR OR OBTAINED THROUGH NON-MEMBERS

These provisions (paragraphs 3.0–3.2) are designed to ensure that two main requirements are met:

1 Member firms should not seek to obtain work via third parties using techniques which they themselves would not be permitted to use.
2 Professional accountancy firms who are asked to carry out work for the clients of non-professional firms should not allow the margins of who does what to be fudged, and, in particular, should take appropriate steps (3.1) to ensure that they are not guilty of rubber-stamping the audit report on accounts prepared by others, and to make it quite clear to all parties that they are carrying out their legal and technical auditing responsibilities.

Relevant Queries

Q1 *The guidance (paragraph 2.1 of Statement 1.209) provides that a member should not allow a non-member to use the same telephone number as his or her own 'without the distinction between the two firms ... being made abundantly clear'. Does that mean that a firm and a non-member body cannot, in fact, have the same telephone number?*

A1 Not necessarily. It would be acceptable for calls to be answered with the number alone, leaving the enquirer to indicate whom precisely he wished to contact.

Q2 *My firm of chartered accountants carries out audit and 'independent accountant' work for half a dozen small companies whose accounts are produced by a firm of unqualified accountants, who also carry out some subcontract work in respect of certain of my smaller clients. Is there any way in which all the relevant services can be billed through one firm - either mine or the unqualified firm – without the need for several invoices which the clients find confusing? (Both firms occupy adjoining premises in the same office block, but the names and telephone numbers are different.)*

A2 Starting at the end, the guidance (paragraphs 2.0 and 2.1 of Statement 1.209) requires you to conduct your firm so that it could not be confused with the non-member firm. Names which are clearly different, and separate telephone numbers, should enable you to meet this requirement.

As to the billing, the guidance (paragraphs 3.1(d) and 3.2 of the Statement) advises that:

(a) you should 'in appropriate circumstances' render your own fee account to the client; and

(b) you should *always* render your own fee account, direct to the client, in relation to *audit* work.

The billing of subcontract work depends on the arrangements that you have with the subcontractor, but in any event should avoid misleading the client. So far as reporting as an 'independent accountant' under the recent statutory exemptions is concerned, you would be wise to treat such work as equivalent, for all practical purposes, to audit – that is, you should bill the client direct.

You enquire as to the possibility of submitting a joint or omnibus account. Paragraph 3.1(d) of the Statement does allow the possibility of such an account in relation to non-reporting work, e.g. tax consultancy, for another firm's client and paragraph 3.2 only requires, in relation to audit (and equivalent) roles, that you 'should render (your) own fee account'. The latter provision would therefore allow you to furnish a bill to the client for your fees, together with the fees of the non-member firm, subject to the account making quite clear the roles which each firm had undertaken, and the individual charges for them. (As to fees generally, see Statement 1.210.)

CHAPTER 16

Fees

The guidance on fees has been regularly revised over the years, reflecting the view of the accountancy bodies that firms should generally be free to charge what they like, but including increasingly detailed requirements designed to ensure that the client knows what he or she is getting, and how much it is likely to cost.

The Statement (1.210) was last revised in February 1994, but further amendment is possible in the future if the Councils of the UK accountancy bodies approve new guidance on due diligence work and contingent fees (referred to earlier in connection with Statement 1.203, on Corporate Finance Advice). There are six section headings in the Statement, and the best way to consider their provisions – some of which are very detailed – is to take them one by one.

'INTRODUCTORY NOTE'

The quotation marks indicate that this guidance is much more specific than one might expect from the title.

Paragraphs 1.0 and 1.1 set out the basic considerations for charging, which become the subject of positive requirements in the next section, 'Fee quotations and estimates'. It should be noted that the considerations in 1.0 relate to the three different methods of charging (agreement of a specific fee, agreement of a charging basis, or 'in the absence of an agreement, a fee calculated by reference to the custom of the profession'), whereas 1.1 indicates four charging elements or requirements *wherever* 'custom of the profession' is invoked.

Paragraph 1.2 indicates the limits of Institute involvement in relation to fees, that is:

● It does not set charge-out rates.
● It does not prescribe the basis for calculating fees (save as provided by 1.0 (above)).
● It does not 'ordinarily investigate complaints relating solely to the quantum of fees' – although, as we shall see, there are ways in which the Institutes can find themselves drawn in.

● Investment business fees are a special situation governed by the Investment Business Regulations.

FEE QUOTATIONS AND ESTIMATES

Paragraphs 2.0 (principle) and 2.1 (discussion) detail requirements as to the *information* which should be given to a client regarding fees prior to the commencement of any engagement. In one respect, 2.1 appears to set a higher standard than 2.0 – due to the omission of two words. Since 2.0 is the statement of principle, and is in what American accountants call 'black lettering' – that is, bold type – relevant ethics committees have taken the view that the guidance expressed in the earlier paragraph should take precedence:

> **A member should inform a client in writing prior to commencement of any engagement of the basis upon which any fee he proposes to charge that client for his services will be calculated and, on request and where practicable, the level of fees likely to be charged for any assignment.**

This statement is, effectively, repeated, with some additional detail in 2.1. However, the words 'on request' do not appear in 2.1, where the apparent requirement is to 'discuss and explain … where practicable, the estimated initial fee'. The (ICAEW) CAASE (Chartered Accountants Advisory Service on Ethics) Committee has advised that the words 'on request' should be implied here also, and that a member is accordingly not subject to criticism if he or she fails to provide a fee estimate on the basis that the client did not request it.

Paragraph 2.2 advises, in the member's interest, that fee proposals 'should be made only after proper consideration of the nature of the client's business, the complexity of its operation and the work to be performed'. Paragraph 2.3 permits fee undercutting ('low balling' in the vernacular), provided that the client has been given a full and complete understanding of (a) the services to be covered by the fee, and (b) the current and future basis on which fees are to be determined.

AUDIT WORK

Paragraph 2.4 is the latest addition to Statement 1.210, incorporated in response to anxieties expressed by accountants and others as to the prevalent and increasing practice of competitive tendering in relation to audit fees.

Fee undercutting is not of concern just to the accountancy bodies in the United Kingdom and the media commentators; a recent consultation exercise carried out at the instance of ICAEW (the Llewellyn-Smith Working Group) has established that the issue is also of concern to many other professional bodies, both in this country and abroad. The UK professional bodies, in virtually all disciplines, are to some extent subject to the provisions of the Restrictive Trade Practices Act of 1976. The Office of Fair Trading, a creature of the Act, spent the late 1970s and 1980s applying remorseless pressure on the professional bodies, and calling on them to abandon their 'restrictive agreements' (guidance, rules and codes), or be prepared to justify them in the courts.

Under such pressures, the UK accountancy bodies progressively adopted conspicuously liberal standards in relation to practice promotion (see next chapter). They were also constrained to give greater freedom about what their member firms might do by way of charging. Pre-1980 guidance had made it a potential disciplinary offence for a firm to seek or obtain work by deliberately undercutting the fees of the incumbent. That provision – which had proved generally unenforceable in any event – was quietly dropped, to be replaced by provisions like those summarised above, and the last-mentioned paragraph 2.3 in particular.

That liberalisation has made it very difficult indeed for the professional bodies to contemplate introducing fetters on the competitive pricing of accountancy services. Indeed the ICAEW consultation established, *inter alia*, that nobody wanted to introduce additional guidance – additional, that is, to the very recent guidance of paragraph 2.4 of Statement 1.210 – presumably on the grounds that it had proved ineffective in the past, and would be strongly resisted by the OFT in the present.

Paragraph 2.4 concentrates on the dangers to objectivity and to professional standards which might arise from fee undercutting. Firms could be required to demonstrate, where fees were a feature in obtaining *or retaining* work, that:

(a) the work done was in accordance with Auditing Standards; and
(b) the client was not misled as to the basis on which fees for the current year and subsequent years were to be determined.

To that one might add, for the sake of completeness, the two requirements quoted earlier, that:

1 the client should have a full and complete understanding of the services to be covered by the fee (2.3(a)) and
2 the objectivity of the firm doing the undercutting should be maintained.

Note: The ACCA guidance does not currently incorporate the provisions on audit 'low balling'.

FEE INFORMATION AND DISPUTES

This section (3.0) deals with the detailing of fees: 'A member should furnish, either in the fee account or subsequently on request, and without further charge, such details as are reasonable to enable the client to understand the basis on which the fee account has been prepared.' A failure by the member or firm to provide this information does, like any other failure to follow the Guide, render a member liable to disciplinary action. Accordingly, this is one aspect of charging fees in respect of which a complaint to the Institute is possible. Such complaints are in fact quite frequent, since clients have realised that one way of getting the fee issue before the accountant's professional body is to complain of inadequate detailing and/or a refusal to supply the appropriate details. (Another aspect would be a complaint, under paragraphs 2.0 and 2.1 (above) that the accountant had failed to give the necessary initial information as to the basis and so forth of fees.) The section on 'fee information and disputes' also advises that a member should be prepared to justify fees which exceed an initial quotation, estimate or indication 'by more than a reasonable amount', and 'to take steps to resolve speedily any dispute which arises'.

All the UK professional accountancy bodies have procedures for arbitration of fees if both parties request it. Unfortunately, such mutual requests are a rarity (probably less than 100 per year for the whole UK profession) and, consequently, fee-linked complaints – actionable by the bodies or not – form a substantial and indigestible proportion of the complaints received.

Paragraph 3.2 indicates a further prolific environment for fee-related complaints: the exercise by an accountant of a lien on clients' documents in respect of work for which he or she has not been paid, and the (associated) withholding of handover information. (We have noted earlier that ACCA does require its members to provide minimal handover information even if fees are outstanding.) The courts have advised that it is a precondition of the exercise of a lien that the accountant – or other professional – has provided information adequate for the client to understand the basis on which the fees have been charged (*Thaper* v *Singh*, Times Law Reports 7 August 1987). The guidance on detailing of fees which we have considered earlier is, of course, in line with such judicial decisions. Paragraph 3.2 concludes with a requirement for the accountant to 'be prepared to take reasonable steps to resolve any dispute relating to the amount of [his or her] fee', and a reference to the available arbitration services.

This is probably not the place for a discussion of the practicality of resolving fee disputes by reference to arbitration or the courts. Most of the fees disputed fit comfortably within the jurisdiction of the small claims court, but many professional firms feel disadvantaged by their inability to claim costs before such a tribunal. Arbitration is a quicker and less expensive alternative to action in the county court or High Court. Clients may, however, feel that arbitration schemes provided by the professional bodies are likely to 'favour their own'! The Law Society has an adjudication service for the settlement of fee disputes of all sizes, but that is apparently under review because of the expense of the service, and is in any event based on statutory powers to which the accountancy bodies have no equivalent (see Chapters 2 and 3).

PERCENTAGE AND CONTINGENCY FEES

Paragraphs 4.0–4.3 set out the by now well-established principle that: 'Fees should not be charged on a percentage, contingency, or similar basis in respect of audit work, reporting assignments and similar non-audit roles incorporating professional opinions.' The recent addition to this principle is the specific inclusion of 'expert witness assignments' as being unsuitable for such a charging basis. (Such a basis would also, no doubt, render the relevant expert witness very vulnerable to damaging cross-examination!) This is accompanied by a warning that: 'even for other work such methods of charging may be perceived as a threat to objectivity and should, therefore, only be adopted after careful consideration.'

Discussion paragraphs deal with charging in respect of insolvency work (often based on a percentage of realisations or distribution), justification for charging on a contingency basis in relation to such corporate finance situations as management buy-out, and a requirement for disclosure whenever a firm charges on a contingency, percentage or similar basis.

INVESTMENT BUSINESS/ADVERTISEMENTS

This long and miscellaneous Statement concludes with cross-references to the Investment Business Regulations, and the succeeding Statement (1.211) on obtaining professional work, 'relative to the mention of fees in advertisements'.

CHAPTER 17

Obtaining professional work

In less than five years in the mid-1980s the UK accountancy bodies moved from a position of virtual no-advertising to one of virtual liberty, if not licence, for firms to promote their services in any way they wished. The guidance of Statement 1.211 reflects that fundamental change in attitude, which was, of course, largely induced by unremitting pressure from the Office of Fair Trading under the authority of the 1976 Restrictive Trade Practices Act.

LIMITATIONS ON PROMOTIONAL ACTIVITY

In fact, the guidance may be comparatively quickly encompassed if one takes the opposite position to that generally taken by the guidance. That is, to focus on those aspects of promotional activity which are *not* available to UK professional accountancy practices.

The (few) remaining 'no go' areas may be summarised as follows:

1 Methods of promotion not consistent with the dignity of the profession (Statement 1.211, paragraph 1.0).
2 Illegal advertisements, and those not conforming with the requirements of:
   (a) the British Code of Advertising Practice, or
   (b) the ITC and Radio Authority Code of Advertising Standards Practice in that they are not legal, decent, clear, honest or truthful (1.1).
3 Promotional activities that include disparaging references to or disparaging comparisons with the services of others (2.0).
4 Advertisements that make claims of size or quality which cannot be substantiated (2.1).
5 Promotional methods amounting to harassment of a prospective client (3.0).
6 Approaches by way of unsolicited personal visit or telephone call to a person who is not a client *in relation to audit or other financial reporting work* (4.0–4.2).
7 'Cold faxing' or 'other electronic means' (4.3).

Note: The restrictions of items 5 and 6 do not apply in terms to certified accountants, who can use any promotional method that is not 'disreputable'.

Apart from those limitations summarised in the list, a firm is in general free to adopt whatever medium or content it desires. There are, nevertheless, one or two points which warrant special mention.

ADVERTISING FEES

Paragraph 1.4 warns that:

> **If reference is made in promotional material to fees, the basis on which fees are calculated, or to hourly or other charging rates, the greatest care should be taken to ensure that such reference does not mislead as to the precise range of services and time commitment that the reference is intended to cover. Members should not make comparisons in such material between their fees and the fees of other accounting practices, whether members or not.**

The comparatively recent facility for a firm to promote its services by quoting fixed fees, fee rates, or fee discounts continues to produce not so much a rash as an epidemic of complaints, with references to the ethics committees of the bodies, whose consideration has tended to focus on advertisements and so forth that are either misleading or unacceptably vague. Clearly, an offer of a 'saving of 25 per cent' is in conflict with the guidance of paragraph 1.4. However, the committees have hitherto shown themselves sympathetic to advertisements which offer '25 per cent off your last year's accountancy fees' or '30 per cent off our published charging rates' because the basis of such discounts is finite.

The bodies are, however, starting to receive increasing numbers of complaints that advertisements which are based purely on cutting costs are not 'consistent with the dignity of the profession' in that they 'project an image inconsistent with that of a professional person bound to high ethical and technical standards' (1.0). The image of the profession is clearly better served by practice promotion which concentrates on *quality* rather than *price* – as the Llewellyn-Smith Working Group pointed out to ICAEW Council in November 1995.

These complaints reflect, to some extent, aggravation on the part of the users of accountancy services, that is, the directors of companies who have received mailshots emphasising discounted fees. A rather larger number, however, arise from the fact that 'blanket' mailshotting tends to arrive at the registered offices of potential client companies, which are located in a majority of cases on the premises of the company's auditors! Such overtures are therefore subject to criticism in more than one respect: not only do they arouse professional hostility, but they are also wasting their sweetness on the desert air. If they do not finish up in the complaints sections of the professional bodies, they will finish up in the waste bin.

The Committee of CAASE (the ICAEW helpline) has recently revisited discounted fee offers, and concluded that '25 per cent off your current accountancy fees' *is* a comparison with 'the fees of other accounting practices'.

The three final sections of the Statement also deserve some mention.

INTRODUCTIONS

Paragraph 5.0 of the Statement is, perhaps, something of a hangover from the past:

A member should not give or offer any commission, fee or reward to a third party, not being either his or her employee or another public accountant governed by ethical standards, comparable to those observed by members or in the context of investment business another authorised firm, in return for the introduction of a client.

The reference to 'investment business' is a comparatively recent addition to guidance which certainly predates the liberalisation of advertising generally. Despite, however, occasional expressions of concern from accountants and others, the 'prohibition' on sweetening the palm of non-professional 'introducers' remains in place. Indeed it is consistent with the guidance of Statement 1.209 on Associations with Non-members.

The term 'another public accountant' has been construed fairly generously by successive ethics committees, so as to include, for example, data processing organisations and management consultancy organisations. It is unclear whether specialist insolvency practitioners who were not chartered or certified accountants would be so regarded. (Commission or other valuable consideration in exchange for the introduction of insolvency appointments is, of course, prohibited by paragraph 2.0 of Statement 1.202.)

RESPONSIBILITY FOR PROMOTIONAL ACTIVITIES

Paragraph 6.0 of the Statement provides that: 'promotional activities carried out in the name of a firm should be construed as … carried out by the individual principals of that practice, whether carried out personally or through agents.' This provision was introduced to deal with problems encountered in pursuing disciplinary processes against large firms, where the member responsible for a particular promotion might be very junior in the firm, and prosecution of a senior partner could come to grief where the latter was able to demonstrate that he or she had no personal role in the firm's promotional activities.

PROMOTION OF INVESTMENT BUSINESS

The Statement closes (paragraph 7.0) with a reminder that obtaining investment business is governed by the Investment Business Regulations, with particular regulations cross-referenced.

Relevant Queries

Q1   *I am aware of the warning against 'cold-calling' in respect of audit and other financial reporting services. Our plan, however, is to employ a telesales agency to call all businesses on the local trading estate, just saying 'Have you heard of us, we're A.B. & Co., Chartered Accountants. We provide all the usual accountancy services, and would like to send you our brochure. Who should we address it to?' Could there be any objection to that?*

A1   We always warn firms intending to use outside agencies – for example, for telesales – that the firm bears responsibility for the activities of the agency (paragraph 6.0, 1.211) and if the operatives get it wrong, your firm might be answerable to the Investigation Committee. The safest course when you plan to promote services by personal visit or telephone call is to focus on services which are clearly not reporting services, such as tax compliance work. If, whether directly or via the telesales agency, you find yourself in a position of promoting a 'mix' of services, which might appear to include audit, you are acting in conflict with the guidance.

Q2   *We should like your view on our mailshot. The headline is, 'Are you happy with your present accountants?'*

A2   Such a caption is impliedly disparaging of the current appointee, because it invites the answer 'No'!

Q3   *Alright then! We should like to begin our mailshot, 'Are you paying too much tax?'*

A3   I'm afraid that similar wording has been criticised by the Committee of CAASE, since it suggests that the existing adviser may not be doing his or her job. Better to avoid these potentially contentious questions, and use positive statements (which you are able to justify) such as 'Saving tax is our business'.

Q4 *We should like to mailshot prospective clients, alerting them to possible savings in VAT. We plan to detail the possible savings, and then put a PS: 'You only have until the end of next month! Act now or it will be too late!'*

A4 Such promotion may be construed as harassment. There could be no objection to a more sober statement that the last date for taking advantage of the saving is, say, 31 December.

Q5 *A number of our clients are getting bombarded with mailshots from a local medium-sized firm. One was sent out on the 14th of the month before last, one last month, and they have just received one dated 14th inst. Surely this amounts to harassment?*

A5 The ethics committees of all the accountancy bodies have tried to avoid a specific definition of what amounts to harassment – it's a matter of considering all the circumstances. One body said that mailshotting at intervals of six months or more would not be likely to amount to harassment. However, monthly mailshotting of prospective clients is likely to be considered as harassment, on anybody's reckoning, and is accordingly 'reportable' to the Institute. Of course, any client who is disaffected by regular mailshotting only has to write to the firm, and ask to be taken off their mailing list …

CHAPTER 18

The names and letterheads of practising firms

This guidance has changed significantly over the years – though not as much as that on practice promotion (previous chapter)! In particular, it reflects the fact that some mixed firms may now properly describe themselves as 'Chartered Accountants' (or 'Certified Accountants'), and former prohibitions about the inclusion of the names of non-members on the letterheadings of member firms have now gone.

As with the previous Statement, it may provide a useful 'gloss' on Statement 1.212 to list those elements which are *not* acceptable in (first) names and (second) letterheadings.

UNACCEPTABLE NAMES

These should not:

1 Conflict with the dignity of the profession (Statement 1.212, paragraph 1.2).
2 Be misleading (1.3), for example by claiming to be 'international' or to have 'associates' where this is not demonstrably the case (1.4).
3 Create confusion with the name of another firm, *even if the members of the practice could lay justifiable claim to that name*.
4 Bear the same name as a trading group (1.7) – although there is no objection to the firm practising under its own name 'as a member of (XYZ) accountancy group'.

Points to note include the acknowledgement that a firm's name based on the names of past or present members of the firm, or a merged or amalgamated firm, is not likely to offend.

LETTERHEADS

The following are potentially objectionable:

1 'Chartered Accountants' as part of the *name* of the firm (as contrasted with the *description*) (2.1); the Registrar of Companies will not, in fact, register the name of a corporate entity which includes 'Chartered Accountants'.

2 Including a description 'Chartered Accountants and (for example) Tax Advisers/Corporate Advisers' (the only acceptable additions to 'Chartered Accountants' are 'Registered Auditors' and 'Licensed Insolvency Practitioners', that is, indicating a right to practise in the relevant reserved area) (2.2).

3 Confusing the names of principals in the firm with others.

4 Confusing the names of chartered accountants (or certified accountants) with others - the former should be distinguished from the latter by the use of designatory letters or otherwise.

5 Including titles, descriptions or designatory letters to which named persons are not entitled.

SEEKING ADVICE

Members in doubt about names or letterheadings are encouraged to consult their Institute.

CHAPTER 19

Second and other opinions

This Statement 1.213 is one of the few (the others are 1.203 and 1.205) which are declared to be of application 'to all members'. Yet the guidance appears very detailed and specific, and is certainly framed from the point of view of auditors and those who may be invited to 'second guess' the advice of auditors.

The guidance commences 'where the opinion of a member, *whether in practice or otherwise*, is sought', and it is certainly desirable that all members should be aware of the dangers and implications of a problem which was first identified on the other side of the Atlantic as *opinion shopping*. The fear evidenced, which became the subject of a request by the DTI to the auditing bodies for investigation, was that a less-than-scrupulous chief executive of a company, having had a difference of opinion with the company's auditors as to the propriety or otherwise of a particular tax or accounting treatment, would in theory be free to go behind the back of the auditor and seek a second opinion about the disputed treatment from what were in practice the auditor's competitors.

If the chief executive succeeded in obtaining a view favourable to his position, then he or she might be able to apply pressure on the audit engagement partner to give way, in the knowledge that if he or she did not do so, his or her firm would probably lose the audit. Alternatively the company might decide peremptorily to discharge the auditor, safe in the knowledge that it had a more favourable opinion in its back pocket. On the other hand, if the second opinion did not meet the company's requirements, then it could seek subsequent opinions – conceivably on the basis of 'massaged' facts – until it achieved one that supported the position it desired.

In a sense the existing guidance on 'additional work' (Statement 1.206, paragraphs 4.0–4.3) makes such a procedure possible because of the provision (paragraph 4.2 of 1.206) that notification to the existing adviser need not be given if the client advanced valid and persuasive reasons for the firm not to do so.

The basic safeguard introduced by the new Statement 1.213 is that the accountant whose (second or subsequent) opinion is sought should 'contact the auditor to provide an opportunity for the latter to bring to his attention any relevant facts and should be prepared, given his client's permission, to provide a copy of his opinion to the auditor'. The relevant paragraph (1.1 of Statement

1.213) concludes: 'If the company or entity seeking the opinion will not permit the member to communicate with the auditor then he should decline to act.'

Paragraphs 1.0–1.2 of the Statement relate to opinions which are 'sought on the application of accounting standards or principles *to specific circumstances or transactions*'. Where an opinion is requested 'on the application of accounting standards or principles relating to *hypothetical* situations and not based on ... specific facts or circumstances of a particular organisation' (paragraph 2.0), the duty of the member is to 'ensure that the nature of the opinion is made clear'.

Since the guidance was introduced there has been a marked absence of publicised problems in this area.

Topic for Discussion/Consideration

The evils identified under the heading of 'opinion shopping' include:

- *a potential threat to the integrity and objectivity of the existing auditor, because of the pressure that the company may bring to bear on him or her to modify his or her original opinion; and*
- *the danger that the accountant whose opinion is 'shopped' will not be in full possession of the facts.*

Are you able to identify any other dangers which might arise from uninhibited use of opinion shopping by the management of client organisations?

CHAPTER 20

Ethics for members in business

BUSINESS MEMBERS

It should be made quite clear that the final Statement in the Guide to Professional Ethics (or equivalent) of the UK accountancy profession is *guidance for business members*. It is not 'business ethics'. This is substantiated by the opening sentence: 'This Statement applies only to Members in Business.'

There is no particular significance in the fact that capital letters are used to denote the relevant category of membership. However, 50 per cent or more of the members of each of the UK bodies are technically 'in business' rather than in, or employed in, practice. Each of the bodies has produced guidance for members in business additional to Statement 1.220, but this is of a technical rather than an ethical nature: for example, Section 1.4 in the ICAEW Hand-book contains a long, technical/legal section on 'Financial and accounting responsibilities of directors' (1.401), and a shorter statement (1.402) on professional conduct in relation to defaults or unlawful acts by or on behalf of the member's employer – the equivalent of Section 1.306 in the guidance for members in practice, already referred to in connection with confidentiality (see Chapter 11).

To return to Statement 1.220 in the Guide to Professional Ethics, it is probably worth noting that the expression 'member in business' is used once more in the introductory section. All other references in the Statement are to 'employed member'. However, the second sentence in the Statement makes it quite clear that the guidance is not for application to members *employed in practice*: 'References ... to an "employed member" include reference to members, whether employed or not, who are engaged in work relevant to their qualification as a member otherwise than in a practising office.'

The introductory section reminds members in business that the Introduction to the Guide, and the Statement 1.205 on Confidentiality are also of application to them. There is, however, no equivalent reminder about Statement 1.203 (on Corporate Finance Advice (see Chapter 11), where, in fact, the only specific reference to members in business is a cross-reference to this Statement!

Members engaged in corporate finance activities, whether in practice or not, would of course do well to make themselves familiar with Statement 1.203 – as with other Statements in the Guide – if only to improve their knowledge of what they might reasonably expect as users of accountancy services.

Following the introductory section, Statement 1.220 divides neatly into two: a section on Objectivity, including 'Financial and other involvement'; and one on Professional and Technical Standards.

OBJECTIVITY

Paragraphs 2.0–2.4 repeat the definition of objectivity in Fundamental Principle 2, and seek to apply it to the 'employed member'.

'Independence' and 'integrity' are also dealt with. Integrity is required in relation to 'any report for which an employed member is responsible' (paragraph 2.2). However, it is made clear, at the beginning of this section that: 'The concept of independence, which is central, to the role of the auditor, has *no direct relevance* to the employed member' (emphasis added). This is a significant step on the road towards the replacement of 'independence' as the core element of accountancy professionalism, with its implication of a freedom from *perceived* threats to objectivity, by the concept of objectivity itself – as we have earlier concluded, a state of mind, but one which may need to be evidenced by conduct. (Earlier guidance for members in business cited the *Alfred Crompton Amusement Machines case*, and dicta by Lord Denning on the independence of employed professionals.)

It is probable that this Statement will require revisiting, to check if Framework principles should apply. CAJEC is, in fact, currently consulting on an extended 'Practical Guidance on Ethical Issues for Members in Business', which would bring all relevant ethics-related guidance into one document, but which also reflects more closely the guidance of the IFAC Code of Ethics for Professional Accountants (see Chapter 23). This may effectively replace Section 1.220 in due course.

For the meantime, it should be noted that there is additional guidance on objectivity in relation to reports for which an employed member is responsible (paragraph 2.2), which may include an element of what the Framework would call *advocacy*, but which should be 'accurate, truthful and within (their) scope, both complete and balanced'.

Employed members are expected to observe the terms of their employment, though these cannot require them to be implicated in dishonest or unlawful transactions (2.3).

The guidance then goes on to deal with 'problems which may be created by financial involvement or personal relationships', particular areas of share dealings and the legal and contractual restrictions to which the employed member may be subject, and receiving gifts – where the guidance is somewhat fuller than its equivalent for practising members (see Chapter 5).

PROFESSIONAL AND TECHNICAL STANDARDS

This section of the Statement (paragraphs 4.0–4.2) amplifies the application of the Fundamental Principles (see Chapter 3) to employed members. A member with sole responsibility for information which is to be made available outside his or her organisation has a duty to ensure that it complies with Fundamental Principle 4 or states fully the reasons for non-compliance (4.1). Where the member does not have sole responsibility, he or she should use his or her best endeavours to achieve the same result (4.2).

The Statement concludes with a warning on 'Status' – which appears to apply to the whole Statement rather than only to the section on professional and technical standards – and a section headed 'Advice', which refers to Institute helplines for members in business – dealt with at greater length in Chapter 22 – and an (ICAEW) insurance scheme in respect of legal fees.

ETHICS FOR MEMBERS IN BUSINESS v. BUSINESS ETHICS

'Business ethics' is one of the growth industries of the late twentieth century! There are university chairs and departments devoted to it. On both sides of the Atlantic, there are learned monthlies and quarterlies whose pages are filled with it. The textbooks on it in the English (and American) language would occupy yards, if not furlongs of shelf space. Related subjects, such as ethical investments and environmental ethics, proliferate. Yet the individual consumer may be no better placed to take advantage of any business ethics *creed* than he or she was twenty years ago.

It is, however, undeniable that a substantial proportion of major business undertakings can point to a 'code', either of their own creation or of a relevant trade association. These codes are likely – as are codes of professional ethics – to include both legal and moral elements. There is of course no enormous credit to be given to someone who wears on his sleeve a requirement which the law imposes on his head! But the requirements of the law are at least *enforceable* against businesses. Enforcement of the non-legal elements of a 'voluntary code' may itself turn out to be voluntary.

As we shall see, enforcement of a professional code is an essential element in every profession's existence and credibility. From that point of view, the code of the world's smallest accountancy regulator – say, the Collegio de Dotores en Ciencias y Contadores of Uruguay, with one of the longest names but only a couple of hundred members – should have more credibility than those of some of the largest trade or industrial associations.

So there is likely to be an essential difference from the aspect of *enforceability* between codes of professional ethics and codes of business ethics. The other major difference is, no doubt, the *purpose* for which the two sets of codes are constructed.

There is no doubt that codes are 'sold' to businesses on the basis that *ethics is good for business*! This is probably true in most cases – although it may not apply to say mining activities in Latin America – but it is hardly an *ethical* reason for accepting a code. Codes of professional ethics should be a statement to the public that 'we are doing this for your good'. There cannot be quite the same authority in a statement which reads 'we are doing this for our own good'!

There is, however, one area in which professional ethics and business ethics should have positive interplay. That is the element which results from the participation of professional accountants and others in businesses when they are themselves subject to higher, published and enforceable ethical standards. They should become 'centres of ethical excellence' in the undertakings which employ them. Although the number of members in business who are referred to the disciplinary processes of the UK professional accountancy bodies is small, when the issues are of sufficient public interest to be considered under the Joint Disciplinary Scheme (see the next chapter), the searchlight focuses with equal intensity on members employed in business and on their professional advisers.

Topics for Discussion/Consideration

1 *Journalism and photography are, at best, 'marginal' professions – and running a newspaper is not a profession at all! Does the fact that the newspaper industry is 'regulated' – with clearly some degree of effectiveness – by the Press Council imply a regime of ethics which is more like professional ethics than business ethics?*

2 *'The Ethical Responsibilities of Members in Business' (ICAEW 1.220) contains no substantive guidance on 'whistle blowing' – which is clearly one of the main issues affecting professionals employed in business. Readers are, however, referred to (ICAEW) Section 1.402, 'Professional Conduct in Relation to Defaults or Unlawful Acts by or on behalf of a Member's Employer'. Is this an area of such importance that it ought to be addressed,*

albeit succinctly, in the Guide to Professional Ethics itself? (More information on practical help for members with such problems is given in Chapter 22. The CAJEC Exposure Draft referred to earlier in this chapter does contain a short summary of the alternatives facing the 'whistle blower'.)

CHAPTER 21

Discipline and enforcement

ENFORCEMENT OF CODE OF CONDUCT

The existence of some sort of code of conduct, and arrangements to enforce that code among members, are two of the elements considered essential for any profession to achieve public recognition. If recognised professions are to retain their credibility, then that enforcement must be seen to be effective.

If any endorsement of the enforcement requirement were needed, it is supplied, for the international accountancy profession, by the Council of IFAC (International Federation of Accountants) (see Chapter 23), which has issued a detailed Statement on Enforcement of Ethical Standards. The UK accountancy bodies, as dutiful members of IFAC, can point to enforcement arrangements that go back to their earliest days, and indeed are referred to in their royal charters.

The IFAC Council Statement does not require a two-stage process of investigation and discipline, but all the UK bodies have such a system. This depends on an Investigation Committee, which receives complaints, investigates them (generally via its secretariat) and decides whether or not something amounting to a prima facie case has been made out. If the Investigation Committee concludes that a case has been made, it will refer what ICAEW calls 'a formal complaint' to the Disciplinary Committee.

The Disciplinary Committee holds regular, 'full dress' disciplinary tribunals, which have comprehensive powers, ranging from fines at the lower end of the scale to suspension or exclusion at the top. In addition, the tribunals can make orders for costs. Some of the bodies have a physical limit on the amount of fine or cost that can be ordered, but ICAEW in particular has recently removed the restrictions.

All the bodies have an Appeal Committee, appeals being generally a re-hearing, but an appeal may be limited, for example to the penalty ordered. In the case of those bodies whose disciplinary tribunals have a discretion as to whether or not to order that their finding be publicised, that order is also usually appellable.

All the bodies provide for a minimum lay-member component in their investigatory/disciplinary committees – usually 25 or 33⅓ per cent.

The powers of some of the bodies include suspension of practising certificate, and, in the case of students, power to declare that an individual is not fit to proceed to membership.

CONTRACT RATHER THAN STATUTE-BASED

As we have seen in the earlier chapters of this text, the powers of the UK accountancy bodies are based on *contract* – that is, members and students accepting such status on the basis of the body's rules and regulations (plus, in the case of the letter, their training contracts) – and not statute. That, in theory, limits the ability of the bodies to pursue offenders.

Various mechanisms are employed by the accountancy bodies to perfect their disciplinary powers in this respect. ICAEW, for example, has the power to retain an allegedly defaulting member in membership, despite the latter's declared intention to resign, and a member seeking admission or readmission is also answerable for breaches committed before he or she came into, or while out of, membership. Non-member principals of firms practising in the reserved areas, or using the description 'chartered accountants', agree to submit themselves to Institute jurisdiction (Affiliates).

There are, in addition, the normal civil law remedies against malefactors who refuse to pay fines and costs – they can be sued by the professional body. In practice, the bodies are unlikely to proceed against members, or former members, where the amounts are small. Non-payment of fines or costs usually imposes its own penalty: automatic expiry of membership.

CONSENT ORDERS

ICAEW, so far alone among the bodies, has found it necessary to offer *consent orders* – generally in relation to minor, technical breaches of regulations, where no member of the public has suffered damage and where the punishment in any event is likely to be minor. It is of course implicit that the member or student has the option of refusing the order, in which case referral to the Disciplinary Committee is inevitable. Many consent orders relate to minor breaches of the Clients' Money Regulations, discovered by the Joint Monitoring Unit in the course of a routine visit to monitor adherence to the investment business regulations.

POWER TO DISCIPLINE FIRMS

All the bodies have power to discipline firms in the reserved areas of investment business authorisation and audit registration. Some have also taken on powers to discipline firms outside these reserved areas. In general terms, however, the bodies will seek to proceed against the individual member or members responsible, partly because that appears more just, and partly because an adverse finding against a firm may have disproportionately serious implications – for example (ICAEW), partners in a disciplined firm who are Council members will not be able to continue as such.

NATURAL JUSTICE

The procedures of all the bodies have, of course, been vetted from the point of view of their adherence to the principles of natural justice, and in particular:

● that 'no man should be a judge in his own court' – including fairness and the full provision to the defendant of information as to any complaint; and
● right of audience – 'audi alteram partem' – the member must be able to defend himself fully against the complaint.

JOINT DISCIPLINARY SCHEME

The Scheme was introduced in the 1970s to deal with complaints against accountants raising issues of public concern. In practice, that usually means complaints where large sums of money are involved.

The Investigation Committee of any of the participating bodies – the three participants are ICAEW, ICAS and ACCA – may certify that in its opinion the circumstances of a case give rise to public concern. The matter will then be referred to the Executive Counsel of the Joint Disciplinary Scheme for enquiry. The detailed enquiry will normally be assigned to a firm of investigating accountants, and recent changes allow the Executive Counsel to direct the investigating accountants as to what they should investigate. (This was not a power which was present in the Scheme as first conceived, and some of the enquiries were, as a result, extremely long and exceedingly costly.) If the investigation gives grounds for a possible adverse finding, the Executive Counsel will ask the Executive Committee – which has responsibility for the overall supervision of the Scheme, and on which all the participating bodies are represented – to appoint a Joint Disciplinary Tribunal.

ACCA has, however, recently given notice that it wishes to detach itself from the Scheme. The public relations implications of such a withdrawal are bad for the profession. All the auditing bodies are currently considering their regulatory regimes with regard to instituting a joint overseeing body, independent to a greater or lesser extent, and ACCA is known to favour something along the lines of a 'General Accounting Council'. Demise of the Joint Disciplinary Scheme would make such an outcome more likely.

The Joint Disciplinary Scheme has its own Appeal Committee, presided over by a retired High Court judge.

It has earlier been noted that an enquiry under the Scheme will look into the activities of all members of any of the bodies, whether they be professional advisers, or officers or employees of companies (or collapsed companies) under investigation. That has, on occasion, led to the disciplining of the officers and employees – although the most severe penalties are usually reserved for defaulting auditors and other professional advisers.

As originally conceived, the Scheme had to refer the ultimate disciplining of members to their own professional body. The Scheme as reconstituted, however, can directly impose any penalty that a relevant participant could impose. Since the issues involved are of public concern, the penalties may be very severe and, in particular, fines may amount to six-figure sums – highly unwelcome even for the largest of firms, not to mention the professional disgrace, which will be widely publicised.

DUTY TO REPORT MISCONDUCT

Alone among the bodies ICAEW has followed the Law Society in implementing a duty upon all members to report serious misconduct. Failure in this duty is of itself grounds for disciplinary action.

The circumstances in which the duty operates are set out in detailed guidance notes (Section 1.113 of the Members' Handbook), and the duty is not triggered unless the circumstances come within the categories set out in GN5 (serious criminal offences) or GN6 (serious breaches of reserved area regulations, gross incompetence, a serious breach of faith in a professional respect, or a serious financial irregularity). The imposition of this duty has led to literally hundreds of additional enquiries to the ICAEW helplines (see Chapter 22).

SCALE OF INVESTIGATIVE AND DISCIPLINARY ACTIVITY

Some idea of the scale of disciplinary activity is given by ICAEW figures of around 3,500 complaints received a year, of which approximately 15 per cent are considered by the Investigation Committee, with nearly half of those becoming 'formal complaints' to the Disciplinary Committee or consent orders. That adds up to approaching two hundred adverse disciplinary findings each year. This figure should be considered in context: even when in the late 1980s the annual complaint level was only of the order of 1,000, the Disciplinary Committee would be likely to 'convict' more than a hundred members a year. (ICAEW firms are now themselves required to have internal complaints procedures as a result of a recently introduced bye-law, which should ultimately reduce Institute complaint levels.)

REVIEWER OF COMPLAINTS

ICAEW also has an independent 'Reviewer of Complaints' – a sort of ombudsman – who can be requested by an unsuccessful complainant to review the decision of the Investigation Committee and, if appropriate, refer the matter back to the Committee with a recommendation that it be reconsidered.

CHAPTER 22

Helplines

This is another area where recent (or current) activity on the international ethics front has been anticipated by long-standing provisions of the UK bodies, all of which have arrangements of a greater or lesser formality for assisting members in relation to ethics and behaviour.

This is in addition to the technical helplines and support provided by all the bodies.

Accordingly it is likely that any pending IFAC standards for member support will be met. In particular, the United Kingdom boasts the first effective helpline for professional accountants in business – the Industrial Members Advisory Committee on Ethics (IMACE), set up by ICAEW in the late 1970s.

ASSISTANCE FOR MEMBERS IN BUSINESS

In setting up the IMACE service, the ICAEW Ethics Committee was conscious that a different approach was needed from the 'volume service' already in place for members in practice. (That volume service is currently marketed under the Chartered Accountants Advisory Service on Ethics (CAASE) title, which deals with more ethical enquiries than any other accountancy body in the world, currently running at 1,000 per month.)

The IMACE service has approximately the same origin in time as the first statements of ethical guidance for members in business. From the beginning it was realised that defining the ethical considerations which apply to such members would be but a fraction of the total support required. The problems and pressures encountered by members in business are, almost invariably, a mixture of ethical issues *combined with* legal, practical, and even *political* aspects, the solution for which requires experience, authority and know-how. The know-how is provided for the IMACE service by a national network of volunteers – senior accountants in industry – who give willingly of their services when requested by the Director of IMACE, a member of ICAEW's Professional Ethics Department.

The procedure is as follows:

1 the member with a problem contacts the Director, IMACE (or in his absence a colleague from the Professional Ethics Department);

2 the Director gives off-the-cuff advice if that is appropriate, and arranges for the member to receive details of the IMACE service – including the fact that it is entirely *confidential*;

3 if the member still requires it, the Director will arrange referral to a local IMACE adviser – having ensured that the latter will have no conflict of interest in advising on the circumstances of this particular case;

4 the member contacts the IMACE adviser to arrange a meeting;

5 the adviser furnishes an (agreed) Note of that meeting to the Director;

6 the member and adviser meet again if that is indicated;

7 the member, having received the advice of the IMACE adviser, is at liberty to follow it, or not, as he wishes.

In the overwhelming number of cases the advice is of course followed. The whole service is absolutely free to the member, the costs being borne wholly by the Institute.

A recent 'extra' is the possibility of up to two and a half hours of legal advice (also paid for by the Institute) with a member of a nationwide Solicitors' Panel. Before being listed on the Panel, the solicitors have to confirm their expertise in the areas of corporate law and corporate crime.

It will be apparent that the service is 'specialist', and costly to run. ICAEW – and those bodies which have duplicated IMACE-type services for their business members, including the Institute of Chartered Accountants of Australia ('MECS') – consider it money well spent. Although the number of enquiries to IMACE grows steadily, it has rarely exceeded 250 enquiries in any one year.

It is interesting to consider the sort of enquiries received by IMACE. These include pressures on members to carry out the following:

● To produce misleading accounts – either to obtain finance or to reduce tax liabilities.

● To placate a regulator or hoodwink investors.

● To suppress benefits-in-kind on the part of the directors.

● To commit other tax offences, involving incorrect P11D forms or forged VAT returns.

● To conceal material information from the board or members of management, or from the company's auditors.

● To allow the company to continue trading whilst insolvent, or to condone fraudulent trading.

● To mask illegal directors' loans or conceal directors' illegal interests and contracts.

● To distort labour charges so as to bolster fees from defence contracts.

● To defraud overseas regimes by improper transfer pricing.

- To sanction bribes to buyers and agents – especially in those countries in which such bribes are the accepted norm.

HELPLINES FOR MEMBERS IN PRACTICE

It has been earlier indicated that these vary considerably in size, formality and throughput. Certain characteristics are (or should be) common to all:

- A well-informed team of advisers, adequate to cope with the number of enquiries received, and able to deal, on the spot, with the vast majority of such enquiries.
- Adequate telephone-answering arrangements, so that the need to return calls is occasional rather than regular.
- Senior secretariat members, combining legal and accountancy skills, to assist with the more difficult query.
- Files and archives to enable the ethical position to be established at least at any time within the past five years, and if possible longer.
- The availability of 'subsidiary' information, such as leaflets, relevant articles, and Help Sheets or similar on popular areas of enquiry.
- An awareness of impending changes to ethical guidance, or other developments which might condition a comprehensive answer to the query.
- Some sort of 'fall back' committee or other agency, able to resolve disputed interpretations of guidance, or to identify issues which need to be incorporated in guidance.
- Liaison in relation to the last-mentioned issues with the professional standard setter, whoever that may be. As an example of such liaison arrangements, the advisory services of the three Institutes of Chartered Accountants in the United Kingdom and Ireland are able to contribute direct to the agenda of CAJEC, the Chartered Accountants Joint Ethics Committee. If CAJEC endorses the need for new guidance, it will make submissions to the Councils of the Institutes – usually after carrying out its comprehensive consultation processes which have been referred to elsewhere.
- Assured confidentiality.

POSITIVE MARKETING

Members are very often shy about consulting the ethical advisory services of their professional body. Accordingly, if those services are to do their job, they need positive promotion among the membership.

I am most familiar with the ICAEW'S CAASE service. It is significant that, when a decision was taken in 1990 positively to promote the helpline for members in practice under the banner 'CAASE' (Chartered Accountants Advisory Service on Ethics) – the helpline had previously had *no* name – the level of enquiries rose by 250 per cent over the next three years.

SUPPORT MEMBERS

By way of further encouragement to shy members, ICAEW has recently set up a network of 'support members' – volunteers in all of the Institute's District Societies. Support members are there to act as a bridge with the Institute's official helplines, to advise members in difficulty – for example, as a result of a monitoring visit – or merely to act as a shoulder to cry on. The scheme has only been in operation for one year, but already something approaching a hundred members have been assisted, who would probably not have approached the Institute in any official way.

Although the Support Member Scheme emphasises the breadth of approach and informality, one practical limitation on support member action is that they are not able to represent defendant members at a disciplinary tribunal. The reason for this is that it would be wrong for the Institute to act as both prosecutor and defender, or to be in danger of being perceived so to act. However the Scheme includes a Register of 'Defendant's Friends' – specialist solicitors and accountants whom members facing disciplinary action can consult, at their own expense.

Support members are, like the secretariats of the Institute's ethics and practice advisory helplines, exempt from the duty to report referred to in the previous chapter.

CHAPTER 23

The international dimension

THE IFAC CODE

As we saw in Chapter 3, the Introduction to the Guide to Professional Ethics sets, in a sense, geographical limits on the application of the Guide, in that:

> **Members in practice overseas are required to comply with local laws and should, in a country in which the profession is controlled by a reputable body, adhere to any local ethical guidance or good practice, even though to do so may not be in accordance with the ethical guidance of the Institute. Members in practice in a country in which the profession is not so guided or controlled should follow the guidance of the Institute unless well-established and generally accepted local practice of reputable firms is to the contrary.**

This provision (paragraph 10) is often referred to as the 'when in Rome provision'.

The International Federation of Accountants (IFAC) has its own Code of Ethics for Professional Accountants which is, in a sense, binding on all the 120 or so IFAC member bodies. The member bodies are bound to do their utmost to implement the standards of the Code within their own country – or at any event, as a minimum, to achieve comparable standards to the Code.

For many years, the UK bodies have regarded themselves as part of an elite. Successive UK representatives to IFAC – and, in particular, its Ethics Committee – have contributed their thoughts, and indeed whole passages, on ethical guidance. The UK bodies have therefore worked on the principle that their standards have always met, and exceeded, IFAC minima.

Interestingly, the above quotation from the Introduction to the Guide exhibits one area in which the UK guidance could be criticised: the IFAC provisions on 'cross-border activities' provide for the maintenance of *IFAC* standards, as a minimum, when a member of a national body provides services outside its domains. Since, however, a growing number of IFAC member bodies have adopted the Code in its entirety, the prevailing local standard is quite likely to be that of IFAC.

The Code is essentially directed at *national member bodies*. However IFAC has produced a form of 'suffix', by which member bodies can confirm that they have adopted the Code in relation to their own members. Everyone with an interest in accountancy ethics should give some attention to the IFAC Code. (It is available from any of the UK and Irish professional accountancy bodies.) In the first instance, it will feature to a greater or lesser extent in the ethical guidance of the vast majority of countries; in the second, it contains some guidance provisions which have no equivalent in the ethical guidance of the UK bodies, for example in relation to some aspects of 'cross-border' activity; and in the third, it may contain elements which will be incorporated in the local guidance in due course – for instance, *confidentiality* is one of the fundamental principles in the IFAC Code.

THE INTERNATIONAL HIERARCHY

At the top is IFAC, with its 120 or so member bodies representing all the developed, and most of the developing, countries of the world.

Below IFAC are a number of regional interest groups, including the Fédération des Experts Comptables et Economiques Européens (FEE), which is a standard setter in its own right – although it has chosen to restrict its activity in technical standard setting. After remaining quiescent for many years, FEE has now produced its position paper on independence and objectivity, based, as we have seen earlier, on Framework principles. A further study is currently underway as to the possibility of creating (or resuscitating) a European Ethics Code. (All that one can say about this is that it is not an immediate prospect, given the pace at which FEE is usually able to operate.)

There are, of course, *international* technical standards, and in particular international *auditing* standards. These have been the subject of an intensive campaign by the International Organisation of Securities Commissions (IOSCO), led by the SEC in New York, to establish international norms for the Audit Report, compliance with which would give an automatic entrée to listing in any recognised stock exchange in the world. That achieved, IOSCO is looking for complementary ethical standards.

IFAC has of course its own committee structure. In full, the list is as follows:

● International Auditing Practices Committee
● Financial and Management Accounting Committee
● Ethics Committee
● Public Sector Committee
● Education Committee.

There is, in addition, an Executive Committee (EXCOM) and a ruling Council. Representation on the Council and the committees is decided at both national and international level – because some countries have, as does the United

Kingdom, more than one interested body.

The UK representation on IFAC (and on FEE) is via the Consultative Committee of Accountancy Bodies (CCAB), set up in response to government pressure following the failure of the bodies to unify in the late 1960s. The six member bodies of CCAB are ACCA, CIMA, CIPFA, ICAEW, ICAI and ICAS. Whichever CCAB body happens to hold the representation at any given time, there is liaison between the bodies in relation to the UK position on IFAC Committees and Council.

In the case of IFAC ethics activity, the liaison body is the CCAB Ethics Liaison Committee. During the life of the IFAC Ethics Committee, the Liaison committee met at least twice-yearly, in advance of the relevant IFAC Committee meeting. However the IFAC Ethics Committee has been very recently disbanded, and replaced by a broader-based 'Forum'. Up to twenty nations will participate in the Forum, which will be held at approximately 15-month intervals. The agenda for the Forum is decided by an Ethics Advisory Group, which met for the first time in September 1995.

CULTURAL DIFFERENCES

The IFAC Code of Ethics acknowledges cultural diversity among its member bodies, and also that some countries will proceed to more sophisticated and developed national guidance than others – at any event in the short term. This is reflected in certain sections of the Code, in particular those dealing with personal relationships:

> **It is recognised that it would be impracticable to attempt to prescribe in detail in ethical requirements the permissible extent of a personal relationship between a professional accountant in public practice and a client or those occupying responsible executive positions ... with a client. Nevertheless, member bodies should advise their members on the kinds of situations which can give rise to the possibility of pressures being exerted on them ... With respect to family relationships it is for each member body to decide, in the light of the social conditions in its own country, what degree of relationship with a client should be regarded as too close to ensure that an independent approach to professional services for that client will not suffer.**

The 'Anglo-Saxon' accountancy culture is, needless to say, well represented on IFAC Council, its committees and other entities. For the purposes of accountancy culture, 'Anglo-Saxon' can be interpreted fairly widely: United Kingdom, Ireland, the United States, Australia, Canada, New Zealand, South Africa, Hong Kong, Zimbabwe, Israel and Egypt, all of whose national bodies are likely to have a similar approach to key issues, such as the provision by audit firms of other services (see Chapters 5–7).

It is perhaps a suitable final thought for this volume that the world of accountancy ethics is well regulated, according to the standards for such things, with an international Code that is both comprehensive and respected. Putting it another way, the language of accountancy is international – and this does not result just from the universality of figures compared with language, nor the scale of activities of the multinational firms. Accounting integrity, objectivity and independence are internationally understood, offering hope of growing, worldwide accordance with these concepts in years to come.

Guide to professional ethics

The following is reproduced, with kind permission, from Section 1.2 of *The Institute of Chartered Accountants in England & Wales Members Handbook 1996*, Volume One.

Section 1.2
GUIDE TO PROFESSIONAL ETHICS

1.200   Introduction and Fundamental Principles

Introduction

Throughout this Guide the term 'member' includes, except where the context otherwise requires, a firm or practice and the term 'partner' includes a director of a body corporate. For the position of affiliates see paragraph 9 below. To make the language of the Guide simpler and more direct the male pronoun is used throughout except at the first reference in each passage when the words 'or she' are added to make it clear that the text refers to all members regardless of gender: the same technique is employed where possessives are used for the first time.

1   In addition to the duties owed to the public and to his or her client or employer a member of the Institute is bound to observe high standards of conduct which may sometimes be contrary to his personal self-interest. This Guide is an aid to members in the identification of occasions upon which they might be at risk of failing to recognise or conform to any of those standards.

2   One of the principal objects of the Royal Charter is to maintain high standards of professional practice and conduct by all members. The Bye-laws render members liable to disciplinary action, *inter alia*, if in the course of carrying out their professional duties or otherwise, they have committed any act or default likely to bring discredit to the member, the Institute or the profession of accountancy. Believing that a high standard of practice and conduct is best maintained by such general provisions, the Council nonetheless considers it desirable to be more explicit in specific areas. Hence this Guide.

Form of guidance
3   Guidance is given in the form of Fundamental Principles and Statements.

The *Fundamental Principles* are drawn from the duties owed by members of the profession, whether in practice or not, and from the requirements of the Charter. They are framed in broad and general terms and constitute basic advice on professional behaviour.

The **Statements** provide more elaboration as to what is expected of members in certain circumstances. They are for the most part in the form of principles (printed in bold typeface) followed by discussion and illustrations.

4 The value of this approach is that it avoids excessive legalism by not having to anticipate every contingency, while at the same time being helpful in giving examples of problem situations.

Guidance not exhaustive
5 Members should be guided, not merely by the terms, but also by the spirit of this Guide and the fact that particular conduct does not appear among a list of examples does not prevent it from amounting to misconduct.

Scope of guidance
6 The *Fundamental Principles* apply to all members. Most of the *Statements* are relevant to members engaged in practice and also, where appropriate, to employees of practising firms but not to other members. Where guidance is relevant to members in business (both employers and employees) this is indicated under the heading to the Statement. For affiliates see paragraph 9 below.

Reserved areas of practice
7 Certain areas of work are reserved by statute to members of the profession who are in practice, whether with other persons or not, namely investment business, insolvency and the audit. In these areas members may be subject to a variety of rules laid down by regulation, breach of which can give rise *ipso facto* to disciplinary proceedings against the member and/or firm. Every effort has been made to harmonise the regulations governing reserved work and the advice contained in this Guide. However, should the advice in this Guide conflict with a regulation, members are bound to follow the regulation.

8 Where an activity within a reserved area is not covered by a legislative provision or where this Guide imposes duties additional to those in a regulation members should follow the advice in this Guide.

Affiliates
9 Affiliates, i.e., non member principals governed by the Regulations concerning affiliates, are bound by the *Fundamental Principles* and, so far as is relevant to practising members, by the *Statements*.

Members in practice overseas
10 Members in practice overseas are required to comply with local laws and should, in a country in which the profession is controlled by a reputable body, adhere to any local ethical guidance or good practice, even though to do so may not be in accordance with the ethical guidance of the Institute. Members in practice in a country in which the profession is not so guided or controlled should follow the guidance of the Institute unless well established and generally accepted local practice of reputable firms is to the contrary.

Students
11 Students, as affirmed by their signature to the training contracts, are bound by the

ethical requirements of the Institute. They also remain bound during the period between the successful completion of the examinations and their admission to membership, at which point, of course, they become subject to the same requirements in their new capacity.

Failure to follow the guidance

12   In determining whether or not a complaint is proved, the Disciplinary Committee may have regard to any code of practice, ethical or technical, and to any regulations affecting member firms laid down or approved by the Council.

13   A member is expected in normal circumstances to follow the guidance contained in the *Fundamental Principles* and in the *Statements* as part of the ethical standards expected of him or her as a chartered accountant. Failure to follow such guidance does not, of itself, constitute misconduct, but in answer to a complaint, a member may be called upon to justify any departure from the guidance.

14   In considering a complaint of misconduct against a member, the Disciplinary Committee may also have regard to the Investment Business, Audit and other Regulations of the Council, the effects of which might otherwise be confined to firms.

Enforcement of ethical standards

15   The power of the Institute to enforce ethical standards is, by the Royal Charter and Bye-laws, entrusted to three standing Committees of the Council, each of which is, in respect of these powers, independent of the Council.

16   The *Investigation Committee* considers complaints against the conduct of members, and is empowered to initiate disciplinary action.

17   If having considered the facts before it, and any representations made by the member, the Committee is of the opinion that in all the circumstances those facts amount to misconduct and is of the further opinion that disciplinary proceedings should be brought, it will prefer a formal complaint to the Disciplinary Committee. Alternatively the Committee may, if it considers that the case does not call for the most serious sanctions and with the member's consent, make certain orders against him. In cases which give rise to or include questions of public concern the Committee may alternatively refer the matter to the Joint Disciplinary Scheme. (See 1.105.)

18   It is the *Disciplinary Committee* or a *Committee of Inquiry* under the Joint Disciplinary Scheme which, alone, can determine, subject to the right of appeal referred to below, whether a complaint of misconduct is proved.

19   From the Disciplinary Committee the member has a right of appeal to the *Appeal Committee*. From a Committee of Inquiry a member has a right of appeal to an *Appeal Committee* of the Joint Disciplinary Scheme.

20   Any failure to follow the guidance in the *Fundamental Principles* or in the *Statements* may also be taken into account by the Committee of the Institute responsible for regulating the work of members and member firms in a reserved area (insolvency, investment business and the audit).

Further advice

21   A member who is in doubt as to his or her ethical position in any matter may seek the advice of this Institute.*

Fundamental Principles

1   A member should behave with integrity in all professional and business relationships. Integrity implies not merely honesty but fair dealing and truthfulness.

2   A member should strive for objectivity in all professional and business judgements. Objectivity is the state of mind which has regard to all considerations relevant to the task in hand but no other.

3   A member should not accept or perform work which he or she is not competent to undertake unless he obtains such advice and assistance as will enable him competently to carry out the work.

4   A member should carry out his or her professional work with due skill, care, diligence and expedition and with proper regard for the technical and professional standards expected of him as a member.

5   A member should conduct himself or herself with courtesy and consideration towards all with whom he comes into contact during the course of performing his work.

---

*A member in public practice, an employee of a practising firm, or a student may consult the Director of CAASE (Chartered Accountants Advisory Service on Ethics).

   A member in business may consult the Director of IMACE (the Industrial Members Advisory Committee on Ethics). See 1.220, *The Ethical Responsibilities of Members in Business.*

1.201 Integrity, Objectivity and Independence

Contents

1.201 Integrity, Objectivity and Independence

Effective: 1 April 1996

The Preface to this Statement applies to all members, together with Section D, Definitions. Sections A, B and C apply only to practising members, affiliates and, where appropriate, employees of practising firms.

Preface

Integrity

1 The Fundamental Principles require that a member should behave with integrity in all professional, business and financial relationships. Integrity implies not merely honesty but fair dealing and truthfulness.

Objectivity

2 Objectivity is essential for any professional person exercising professional judgement. It is as essential for members in business as for practising members. Objectivity is the state of mind which has regard to all considerations relevant to the task in hand but no other. It is sometimes described as 'independence of mind'.

The need for objectivity is particularly evident in the case of a practising accountant carrying out an audit or some other reporting role where his professional opinion is likely to affect rights between parties and the decisions they take.

Framework

3 This Statement provides a Framework within which members can identify actual or potential threats to objectivity and assess the safeguards which may be available to offset such threats. As well as including illustrative guidance, it includes examples of specific threats to objectivity.

Objectivity and independence regarding an auditor

4 **Section A** of this Statement which follows deals with the objectivity and independence required of an auditor. It starts with an analysis of potential threats to an auditor's objectivity and of the safeguards available and continues with detailed guidance relating to specific areas of threat.

Objectivity and independence in other financial reporting roles

5 **Section B** calls for a similar degree of objectivity and independence to be exercised by a member in financial reporting and similar roles outside the audit.

Objectivity in other situations

6 **Section C** deals with situations outside the areas dealt with in Sections A and B where a member must remain conscious of the need to preserve his objectivity and to observe appropriate safeguards so that his judgement is not swayed by considerations of self-interest or other improper factors.

Members in business

7 Objectivity in relation to members in business is dealt with in Statement 1.220, at the end of this Guide.

Conflicts of interest

8 Conflicts of Interest have an important bearing on objectivity and independence. Attention is drawn to the guidance in Statement, Conflicts of Interest (1.204).

Members in practice overseas
9   The attention of members in practice overseas is drawn to paragraph 10 of the Introduction (1.200) to this Guide.

Introduction

1.0   Safeguarding objectivity

1.1   In order to safeguard their objectivity, members should consider certain matters before deciding whether to accept any appointment. The matters to be considered include those under the following headings:

- **The expectations of those directly affected** (and entitled to be affected) by the work.
- **The public interest** and its bearing on the work.
- **The threats to objectivity** which may arise actually or potentially.
- **The safeguards** which are or can be put in place, overt or otherwise, to offset the threats.

These headings are discussed in more detail in the following paragraphs.

1.2   The responsibility for seeing that the above matters are properly considered resides ultimately, in the case of members in practice, with the engagement partner who takes the responsibility for signing the report for the client concerned. Firms should establish reliable procedures to ensure that these matters are properly addressed.

The expectations of those directly affected
1.3   Those directly affected are likely to be concerned about the existence of any relationship or situation affecting a member or firm, or any business or other interest held by the member or firm, which may threaten or appear to threaten objectivity.

Accordingly the member concerned should consider a possible need to disclose the relationship, situation or interest to the affected parties.

The public interest and any bearing it has on the work
1.4   The public interest should be a factor which all members should bear in mind when accepting any assignment or appointment.

Threats to objectivity
1.5   Threats to objectivity can arise in a number of ways, some general in nature and some related to the specific circumstances of an assignment or role. Members should identify the threats and consider them in the light of the environment in which they are working; they should also take into account the safeguards which assist them to withstand threats and risks to their objectivity.

Categories of threats
1.6   Threats to objectivity are discussed in more detail below, but in paragraph 2.1 there are set out some general categories under which threats may be considered. It may prove

helpful to members to categorise the threats because the more clearly the nature of the threat is identified, the clearer it becomes:

● whether the member's own integrity and working environment may be sufficient to offset/mitigate the threat;
● whether specific safeguards should be added;
● if safeguards should be added, which of those would most appropriately address the risk;
● in what circumstances the appearance of risk or conflict becomes so great that there ought to be a refusal to act.

The easiest way of avoiding such threats would be for members to decline to act in any circumstances where the slightest threat to objectivity might exist. This could, however, deny to clients and employers proper access to a member's breadth of professional expertise and knowledge of the client's or employer's business, and, in deciding whether to include such a prohibition in its guidance, the Institute always bears in mind the need to maintain a balance that respects the interests of clients and employers and the possible wider public interest.

2.0 Section A – Objectivity, independence and the audit

Threats to objectivity

2.1 Threats to objectivity might include the following:

The self-interest threat

2.2 A threat to the auditor's objectivity stemming from a financial or other self-interest conflict. This could arise, for example, from a direct or indirect interest in a client or from a fear of losing a client.

The self-review threat

2.3 The apparent difficulty of maintaining objectivity and conducting what is effectively a self-review, if any product or judgement of a previous audit assignment or a non-audit assignment needs to be challenged or re-evaluated in reaching audit conclusions.

The advocacy threat

2.4 There is an apparent threat to the auditor's objectivity, if he becomes an advocate for (or against) his client's position in any adversarial proceedings or situations. Whenever the auditor takes a strongly proactive stance on the client's behalf, this may appear to be incompatible with the special objectivity that audit requires. (And see paragraphs 4.67 et seq. (below).)

The familiarity or trust threat

2.5 A threat that the auditor may become over-influenced by the personality and qualities of the directors and management, and consequently too sympathetic to their interest. Alternatively the auditor may become too trusting of management representations so as to be inadequately rigorous in his testing of them – because he knows the client too well or the issue too well or for some similar reason.

The intimidation threat

2.6 The possibility that the auditor may become intimidated by threat, by dominating personality, or by other pressures, actual or feared, by a director or manager of the client or by some other party.

Each of the above threats may arise either in relation to the auditor's own person or in relation to a connected person such as a member of his family or a partner or a person who is close to him for some other reason, such as past or present association or obligation or indebtedness. These aspects of the potential threats are explored in the detailed guidance of paragraphs 4.50 to 4.52.

3.0 Safeguards which are available to offset the threats

3.1 Auditors should always consider the use of safeguards and procedures which may negate or reduce threats. They should be prepared to demonstrate that in relation to each identified threat, they have considered the availability and effectiveness of the safeguards and procedures and are satisfied that their objectivity in carrying out the assignment will be properly preserved.

3.2 Safeguards and procedures

The safeguards and procedures might include:

3.3 *Factors in the environment of the practice which will operate so as to offset any threat to objectivity*

An exhaustive list of these countervailing factors is not possible, but auditors should expect where possible to have developed the following characteristics in their firms. Where they have been developed they will provide safeguards.

(i)   Chartered accountants are taught from the outset of their training contracts to behave with integrity in all their professional and business relationships and to strive for objectivity in all professional and business judgements. These factors rank highly in the qualities that chartered accountants have to demonstrate prior to admission. They should therefore be well used to setting personal views and inclinations aside.

(ii) Engagement partners should have sufficient regard for their own careers and reputations to be encouraged towards objectivity and to effective use of safeguards.

(iii) Within every firm there should be strong peer pressure towards integrity. Reliance on one another's integrity should be the essential force which permits partners to entrust their public reputation and personal liability to each other.

(iv) Firms should set great store on their reputation for impartiality and objectivity. It is the foundation for their ability to practise and to gain work over the medium and long term, and they should not permit a member of the firm to risk it for short term benefit or gain.

(v)   Firms of all sizes should have established strong internal procedures and controls over the work of individual principals, so that difficult and sensitive judgements are reinforced by the collective views of other principals, thereby also reducing the possibility of litigation.

3.4 *Safeguards and sanctions built into the structure of the profession itself*
These might include:

(i) The long-standing ethical code of the profession, of which this guidance forms part. Where appropriate, this code imposes specific prohibitions where the threat to the auditor's objectivity is so significant, or is generally perceived to be so, that no other appropriate safeguards would be effective.

(ii) The ethical support provided by the Institute, including the CAASE* ethical helpline, published advice on ethics such as Help Sheets, and the Support Member Scheme involving District Societies.

(iii) The reinforcement given to the above safeguards by a policing system which reacts to complaints, whether by members of the public or members of the profession, investigates the background to the complaints, and where necessary commences disciplinary proceedings against an offending member. Together with monitoring (below), the system ensures that a firm's past conduct and current procedures are likely to come under close independent professional scrutiny if the conduct of practising members gives rise to challenge over their exercise of these guidelines.

(iv) The active monitoring procedures conducted by the profession for reserved activities such as auditing. On behalf of the Institute Committees concerned, the Joint Monitoring Unit visits firms which are registered to conduct audits. It examines firms' compliance with the Audit Regulations and reports to those Committees. The Regulations embrace in their requirements the whole of this guidance.

3.5 *Steps taken by firms to ensure that threats to objectivity are recognised, documented and mitigated*
These might not be disclosed to outsiders unless disciplinary or regulatory follow-up requires it. Examples of internal procedures within firms which may contribute to reassurance that the required audit objectivity has been preserved include:

(i) Arrangements to ensure that staff are adequately trained and empowered to communicate any issue of objectivity that concerns them to a separate principal.

(ii) The involvement of an additional principal (in the case of a sole practitioner, a qualified colleague) to carry out a review or otherwise advise. (See 3.6 below.)

(iii) Rotation of engagement partners and staff.

(iv) The evaluation of a potential client when a firm is approached to act, to assess such facts as the integrity of the client's management, company profile, accountancy competence, etc.

(v) Formal consideration and review of the continuance of all engagements before the firm's name is allowed to go forward for reappointment as auditor.

*Chartered Accountants Advisory Service on Ethics

(vi) An overall control environment, starting with a professional approach towards matters of quality and ethics, and taking in staff training, development and performance appraisal, and the assurance provided by a regularly monitored and evidenced control system.

3.6 *Review procedures*
(i) Wherever the review procedures indicate that an audit assignment should be accepted or continued only with additional safeguards against loss of objectivity, the engagement partner's decision and the range of safeguards appropriate to the assignment should be subject to independent review by a partner unconnected with the engagement.

(ii) The safeguards to be applied should include, as appropriate, rotation of the audit engagement partner and of senior audit staff. In particular the firm should review annually the possible need for rotation of an audit engagement partner.

(iii) It is a useful practice to keep records of all reviews carried out.

3.7 *Sole practitioners and small firms*
(i) Not all the safeguards suggested in the course of the preceding guidance will be available to the sole practitioner within his or her firm. The practitioner should therefore set up alternative standing arrangements to consult externally with another member or with Chartac Practice Services. Where the arrangements are with another practitioner they could include provisions as to the maintenance by the latter of client confidentiality and an undertaking not to accept instructions from any client whose work is the subject of review for a period of two years thereafter.

(ii) To the extent that a small firm may find difficulty in implementing the safeguards principals should set up external consultation arrangements appropriate to their particular circumstances.

(iii) Where the practitioner's own review indicates that an audit engagement should only be accepted or continued with additional safeguards to protect the practitioner's independence, he or she should undertake such consultation before proceeding further. The extent of the consultation will vary according to the nature of the problem; in some cases it may be confined to a discussion of principles; in others it may involve an examination of the file or a discussion of personal relationships.

(iv) A sole practitioner should not accept or continue appointment as auditor of a company at a time when he is trustee of a trust holding shares in that company, unless he has made arrangements for such consultation. (See paragraph 4.46 below.)

3.8 *The involvement of a third party such as a client audit committee, or a regulatory body or another firm*

3.9 *Refusal to act where no other course can abate the perceived problem*
Some exclusions and prohibitions are the subject of statute or regulation outside the

control of the profession. In addition, there are some situations in which the threat to an auditor's objectivity is so significant, or generally perceived to be so, that an auditor should, having regard to preservation of the public image of his profession, decline to accept appointment, even if he believes that the circumstances are such that available safeguards and procedures could, in his particular case, enable him to maintain proper objectivity. In this eventuality, he should decline or resign appointment.

3.10 It follows from the preceding paragraphs that the perception of the public (or any section of it) that an auditor's objectivity may be threatened is not, of itself, a reason why an appointment should be refused. The countervailing pressures and safeguards described above may often override a threat. Members and firms are encouraged to make clients and others outside the profession aware of the extensive and sophisticated compliance procedures that they employ.

4.0 Guidance on specific areas of threat

Area of risk – undue dependence on an audit client

4.1 If the recurring fees from a client company or group of companies constitute a substantial proportion of the fee income of an audit firm, a self-interest threat is likely to arise, so as to imperil objectivity.

4.2 Accordingly a member should not accept an audit appointment or similar financial reporting assignment from an entity which regularly provides him, his firm or an office within the firm with an unduly large proportion of his or its gross practice income. An unduly large proportion would normally be 15 per cent, or, in the case of listed or other public interest companies defined in paragraphs 7.6 and 7.7 the appropriate figure would be 10 per cent.

4.3 In the case of a member practising part-time, the relevant proportions are 15 per cent and 10 per cent of the member's gross *earned* income.

4.4 A new firm seeking to establish itself, or an established firm reducing its activities may not be able to comply with the above criteria, at any event in the short term. Such firms should take particular care to implement the safeguards referred to below.

4.5 The fees from a number of one-off assignments could contribute to a problem of undue dependence. One-off assignments which by their special and repetitive nature become regular assignments should be regarded on the same basis as recurring fees.

4.6 Where a member is dependent for his income on the profits of any one office within a firm and the gross income of that office is regularly dependent on one client or a group of connected clients for more than 15 per cent (in the case of listed or other public interest companies 10 per cent) of its gross fees, a partner from another office should take final responsibility for any report.

4.7 While the overall criteria set out in paragraph 4.2 do not indicate the presence of a serious threat, individual engagement partners may be faced with a personal threat because their personal portfolio is dominated by a single client, on whom they might become so dependent as to lose objectivity.

Safeguards in relation to undue dependence on an audit client
4.8   It is the responsibility of both the audit engagement partner and the management of the firm to ensure that in such situations additional safeguards are introduced by way of review and second partner support to ensure that objectivity of judgement is retained by the partner responsible for engagement decisions and audit judgements.

4.9   The figures in paragraph 4.2 above indicate only the extremes beyond which the public perception of a member's objectivity is likely to be at risk. It is the duty of the firm regularly to satisfy itself that it is not open to criticism in respect of any audit engagement, having regard to all the circumstances of the case. For this purpose a firm should, before accepting an audit appointment and as part of its annual review (see paragraphs 3.2 to 3.7 above), carefully consider against the criteria set out in this Statement the propriety of accepting or retaining each audit client or group of connected clients, the fees from which for audit and other recurring work, excluding one-off assignments, represent 10 per cent or more of the gross practice income or of the gross earned income of a member practising part-time. In the case of a listed company or other public interest company – see paragraphs 7.6 and 7.7 (Definitions) – a figure of not more than 5 per cent is the appropriate point to initiate review.

Area of risk – loans to or from a client; guarantees; overdue fees
4.10   **A self-interest threat will arise if an audit firm or any principal of the firm should directly or indirectly make any loan to, or receive a loan from a client, or give or accept any guarantee in relation to a debt of the client, firm or principal.**

4.11   An audit firm or a principal of the firm should not receive any loan from a client. This is because the size of the perceived self-interest threat arising in such circumstances is generally seen as being too great to be offset by any available safeguards. Nor should a firm or principal make any loan to a client, although this restriction does not normally apply to any account in credit with a client clearing bank or similar financial institution.

4.12   Paragraph 4.11 above is not intended to preclude a loan, overdraft or home mortgage being accepted from an audit client financial institution in the normal course of business and on normal commercial terms by a principal or employee, unless:

(a)   the loan is applied so as to subscribe to partnership capital; or

(b)   the principal is an engagement partner in relation to the client.

Overdue Fees
4.13   Similar considerations apply where there are significant overdue fees from a client or group of connected clients.

Safeguards in relation to overdue fees
4.14   Before work is commenced on an audit where there are overdue fees, a review of the situation should be undertaken by a principal not involved in the audit, to ascertain whether the overdue fees, taken together with the fees for the current assignment, could be regarded as a significant loan.

Area of risk – hospitality or other benefits
4.15 A self-interest threat arises where anyone in the firm receives a benefit by way of goods or services, or hospitality from a client. These should not, therefore, be accepted by a firm or by anyone closely connected with it unless the value of any benefit is modest.

Area of risk – actual or threatened litigation
4.16 Where litigation takes place, or appears likely to take place, between an audit firm and a client, both a self-interest threat and an advocacy threat may arise.

4.17 These threats are likely to call into question the objectivity of the auditor and his ability to report fairly and impartially on the company's accounts. At the same time the existence of such action or threat of action could affect the willingness of the management of the company to disclose necessary information to the auditor.

4.18 The issue by the audit client of a writ for negligence against the auditor would be considered to impair the latter's objectivity. The inclusion in any litigation of allegations against the client of fraud or deceit made by the auditor may also impair objectivity. Such impairment may not necessarily result when the litigation arises solely out of a fee dispute.

4.19 It is not possible to specify precisely the point at which it would become improper for a firm to continue as auditors. However, a firm should have regard to circumstances where litigation might reasonably be perceived by the public as in contemplation, e.g. where publicity is given to matters adversely affecting a listed or other public interest company and reference is made to the company's reliance on accounts or other financial statements prepared by the firm.

Area of risk – participation in the affairs of a client
4.20 Participation in the affairs of a client is likely to lead to self-interest threats which are either in practice too great to be overridden by available safeguards, or are likely to appear so to interested parties.

4.21 There may be statutory prohibitions on a firm acting as auditor. For instance the Companies Act 1989, Section 27, prohibits an officer or employee of a company, or a partner or employee of such a person from accepting appointment as auditor of that company.

4.22 In general, no principal or employee of an audit firm may be an officer or employee of a client, and should not have held such a position in a period so closely preceding the firm's appointment as to constitute a significant threat of self-interest or of self-review.

4.23 Self-interest threats can also arise if an officer or senior employee of an audit client is a close connection of a principal of the audit firm. For the purposes of this paragraph only, the definition of 'closely connected' (see paragraphs 7.2 to 7.5 (below)) includes additionally adult children and their spouses, brothers and sisters and their spouses, and any relative to whom regular financial assistance is given or who is otherwise indebted financially to the principal.

4.24 A member should not personally take part in the conduct of the audit of a company if he or she has, during the period upon which the report is to be made, or at any time in the two years prior to the first day thereof, been an officer (other than auditor) or employee of that company.

4.25 A firm should not report on a company if a company associated with the firm fills the appointment of secretary to the company. There is no objection to the firm providing assistance to the company secretary.

Area of risk – principal or senior employee joining client
4.26 The objectivity of a firm reporting on a company (or other entity) may be threatened, or appear to be threatened, if an officer of the audit client has been a principal or senior employee of the firm.

4.27 Threats to the firm's objectivity of a self-interest nature may arise where there remain significant connections between the officer and his former firm, and appropriate action should be taken to ensure that objectivity is not impaired. For example:

(a) the officer should not derive retirement or other benefits from the firm unless these are made in accordance with predetermined arrangements that cannot be influenced by any remaining connections between the officer and his former firm. In addition any amount owed should not be such as to appear likely to threaten the firm's objectivity; and

(b) the officer should not participate or appear to participate in the firm's business or professional activities. Inclusion on the notepaper of the firm is an indication of such participation and the provision of office accommodation or secretarial or information technology support by the firm may indicate such participation.

4.28 Additionally, the firm's objectivity may be threatened because of participation in the conduct of an audit by a principal or senior employee in the knowledge that he is to join the client.

Safeguards in relation to principal or senior employee joining audit client
4.29 The firm should therefore make appropriate provision in its procedures for further safeguards to include the following:

(a) a requirement for immediate notification to the firm by a principal or senior employee involved in a client's audit of the intention or any discussions concerning the possibility of joining the client;

(b) where the individual is to join the client or is involved in substantive negotiations with the client, the removal from the audit team of any such principal or senior employee coupled with a review of any significant audit judgements made by such principal or senior employee.

Area of risk – mutual business interest
4.30 A mutual business interest with a client company or with an officer or employee of the company will create a self-interest threat. Where such an interest

is an element of an engagement, the engagement should not be accepted or continued unless appropriate safeguards can be set up within the firm – see paragraphs 3.2 to 3.8 above.

Area of risk – beneficial interests in shares and other investments

4.31 Any beneficial interest on the part of a principal or anyone closely connected with a principal of the audit firm in a client company will constitute an insurmountable self-interest threat.

4.32 Where an employee, or a person closely connected with an employee, has such a beneficial interest, the employee should not take part in the audit of the client company.

4.33 A beneficial interest is a beneficial shareholding or other direct investment in the company (and see paragraph 7.9).

4.34 Paragraph 4.31 above is not intended to preclude a principal or a person closely connected with a principal from holding or continuing to hold, in the normal course of business and on normal commercial terms, an insurance or pension policy with a client insurance company or society, though an engagement partner should not take out a new policy with such a client.

4.35 Nor is a beneficial holding in an authorised unit or investment trust, or Lloyd's syndicate which holds shares in a client company so precluded.

4.36 A principal in an audit firm should not have a Personal Equity Plan which has among its investments any audit client. However he may have a Personal Equity Plan which invests solely in unit trusts or in an investment trust, provided that the firm does not report upon the trust.

4.37 Where a principal inherits shares or marries a shareholder, or a relevant investment occurs as a result of a takeover, the investment should be disposed of at the earliest practicable date, being a date at which the transaction would not amount to insider dealing. Similar action should be taken where a beneficial investment is held in a company becoming an audit client. Where the necessary disposal cannot be achieved within the timescale envisaged the firm should not continue as auditor.

4.38 Where a provision in the Articles of Association of a company or an Act of Parliament requires the auditor to be a shareholder the auditor should hold no more than the minimum number of shares necessary to comply with that provision in the Articles or with the Act, and the shareholding should be disclosed in the accounts, in the Directors' Report or in the Audit Report.

Area of risk – beneficial interests in trusts

4.39 A beneficial interest in a trust having a shareholding in an audit client company should be regarded as a beneficial interest in that company and be subject to similar considerations as in 4.31 above.

4.40 Where a principal or a person closely connected with a principal holds a beneficial interest and the principal is and wishes to remain a trustee, the shareholding should be regarded as equivalent to a beneficial shareholding, and the practice should cease to report.

4.41 Where the principal or a person closely connected with him holds the beneficial interest in a trust, and where the principal is not a trustee, he should cease personally to take part in the audit of the company as soon as he becomes aware of the shareholding.

Area of risk – trusteeships
4.42 If a principal or employee of the firm or a person closely connected with either acts as a trustee of a trust which holds shares in a client company, a self interest and/or familiarity threat will arise. The threat to objectivity is patent where the shareholding is in excess of 10 per cent of the issued share capital of the company or of the total assets of the trust.

4.43 Where the trust holds shares in a listed company or other public interest company (see paragraphs 7.6 and 7.7 (Definitions)) and the holding is in excess of 10 per cent of the issued share capital of the company, or the trust's aggregate investment in the company exceeds 10 per cent of the total assets comprised in the trust, the firm should not accept or continue appointment as auditors. The shareholdings (in relation to the issued share capital of the company) of trusts of which principals or members of staff of the firm are trustees should be regarded as aggregated for the purposes of this paragraph.

4.44 The restrictions and aggregations contained in paragraph 4.43 above do not necessarily apply in the case of staff member trustees, where the trust is of a personal or family nature and is not client-related.

4.45 In the case of companies other than listed companies and public interest companies the 10 per cent limits do not apply, but appointment should not be accepted unless appropriate safeguards are implemented.

Safeguards in relation to trustee holdings
4.46 These include the following:
(a) A trustee, or someone with whom a trustee is closely connected (see paragraph 7.2 et seq.) should not act as the principal or person responsible for the audit of the company in which the trust is a shareholder.

(b) A sole practitioner should not accept or continue appointment as auditor unless he is able to arrange for the consultation referred to in paragraph 3.7 (above), and that consultation confirms the propriety of accepting or continuing appointment.

(c) The disclosure of the trust investment in the accounts, in the Directors' Report or in the Audit Report, save in the case of trustee shareholdings where the aggregate of all relevant shareholdings is less than one per cent of the issued capital of the company.

(d) Where a close personal relationship develops in the course of a trustee shareholding, a member should have regard to the review procedures recommended in paragraphs 3.2 to 3.7 (above).

4.47 Similar considerations apply when a person closely connected with the firm is a director or employee of a trust company which acts as trustee of a trust holding investments in a company on the accounts of which the firm reports.

Area of risk – nominee shareholdings; 'bare trustee' shareholdings
4.48 Similar considerations to those applying to trustee shareholdings (see paragraph 4.42 *et seq.*) apply also in the case of nominee shareholdings and 'bare trustee' shareholdings.

Area of risk – voting on audit appointments
4.49 Where a principal or employee of the audit firm holds shares in any capacity in an audit client company, those shares should not be voted at any general meeting of the company in relation to the appointment, removal or remuneration of auditors, because to do so would give rise to a patent conflict of interest.

Area of risk – connections; associated firms; influences outside the practice; employees
4.50 It should be recognised that each of the threats dealt with in paragraphs 2.1 to 4.49 may arise either in relation to a principal of the firm, or in relation to a close connection such as a member of his immediate family (see paragraphs 7.2 to 7.4 below). Threats can also arise because of pressures exerted upon a firm by an associated firm or an outside source introducing business, such as bankers, solicitors, or government.

4.51 The threat to objectivity will depend upon the closeness of relationships and associations, the strength of an associate's interest in the firm's retaining a client, and the extent to which the introduction of business by an outside source is able to affect the firm's fee income.

4.52 The audit firm should not employ any person on the audit who would by any of the foregoing principles be personally excluded from the role of auditor.

Safeguards in relation to connections etc.
4.53 The possibility of a threat to objectivity arising in such circumstances should be borne in mind and provided for in the firm's review machinery. All the safeguards listed in paragraphs 3.2 to 3.9 (above) are of potential relevance.

4.54 It should be borne in mind that the threat to objectivity will be less where any connection is with a junior member of staff or with a member of the firm who is not personally engaged on the audit in question, and where his or her office is distant from the office conducting the audit.

Area of risk – provision of other services to audit clients
4.55 There are occasions where objectivity may be threatened or appear to be threatened by the provision to an audit client of services other than the audit. All the safeguards described in paragraphs 3.2 to 3.9 may have an application to the provision of other services.

4.56 There is no objection to a firm providing advisory services to a company which are additional to the audit. Care must be taken to ensure not to perform management functions or to make management decisions. It is economic in terms of skill and effort for professional accountants in public practice to be able to provide other services to their clients since they already have a good knowledge of their business. Many companies (particularly smaller ones) would be adversely affected if they were denied the right to obtain other services from their auditors.

4.57 The threats that may arise in the course of providing other services are discussed in the remainder of this section. The threats may be analysed under the headings set-out in paragraph 2.0 above.

The self-interest threat
4.58 All work that creates a financial relationship between the auditor and the audit client may appear to create a self-interest threat – as does payment for the audit itself. The nature of the threat sometimes perceived is that the auditor's objectivity might be impaired by a need to remain on good terms with the directors of the audited company in order to preserve a working relationship. The perceived threat grows with the size of the fees and is thus increased by work or services additional to the audit. But the most significant dimension of any threat, real or perceived, is likely to reside in the size of the total fees earned from a client in relation to the whole fees of the firm. This threat is addressed by the guidance as to undue dependence in paragraphs 4.1 to 4.9 (above).

The self-review threat
4.59 Audit work itself gives rise to self-review. The auditor reviews matters that he has previously judged in prior-year audits, matters that were judged at planning stage, his recommendations (or lack of them) to management at previous audits, etc. In auditing perhaps more any other activity there is a need for a readiness to recognise and avoid past mistakes. The auditor must adopt the objectivity and independence of mind to be able to acknowledge past errors or mistakes of judgement and report fairly and afresh.

4.60 The provision of other services may give rise to further needs for self-review. If, for example, the firm has designed or recommended any part of the systems or controls on which the audit relies, the audit team will need to take particular care to ensure that the audit judgements are objective, perhaps in the case of larger firms by arranging that there is little or no common membership between the systems work and the audit team.

4.61 If, as is common for smaller companies, the auditor has prepared any of the data contained in the financial statements or drafted material for the notes, or assisted in the preparation of the accounting records, a degree of self-review arises.

4.62 There is a spectrum of involvement by the auditor in the preparation of accounting records. It ranges from the situation prevailing in small companies where the auditor may prepare much of the accounting records and the financial statements as well as auditing them, to the other end of the spectrum where in the case of a major listed company the auditor does not participate in any part of the preparation process. Even in the latter case, the auditor who detects omissions in the company's proposed disclosures will normally suggest and draft the amendments required, so that in the end it is uncommon for a set of financial statements to appear where the auditor has had no hand whatsoever in the presentation or drafting.

4.63 These processes of assistance, entailing self-review as they do, are not intrinsically damaging to audit objectivity, but pose a threat to it. Safeguards are necessary.

4.64 At the smaller company end of the spectrum the safeguards reside in a considered analysis by the auditor of the work done in preparation of records and statements and careful consideration as to what separate audit procedures and scope are thus required. At the other end of the spectrum, in the case of a listed company or other public interest company audit client (see paragraphs 7.6 and 7.7 Definitions), an audit practice should not participate in the preparation of the company's accounts and accounting records save in relation to assistance of a routine clerical nature or in emergency. Such assistance might include, for example, work on the finalisation of statutory accounts, including consolidations and tax provisions. The scale and nature of such work should be regularly reviewed.

Specialist valuations as an example of the self-review threat
4.65   The provision for an audit client of specialist valuation services which directly affect amounts in the financial statements gives rise to a clear self-review threat to objectivity.

4.66   A firm should not audit a client's financial statements which include the product of a specialist valuation (see paragraph 7.10) carried out by it or an associated firm or organisation in the same country or overseas.*

The advocacy threat
4.67   Advocacy arises where a practitioner becomes an advocate for a client's position in any adversarial proceeding or situation. There is nothing improper about a position of advocacy, and many types of professional services and support to a client may require it.

4.68   Advocacy in a simple sense is always present where a firm supports its clients' interests. At the same time, a professional person is always required to strive for objectivity in all professional work (see Fundamental Principle 2 in the Introduction and Fundamental Principles (1.200 above)).

4.69   But advocacy can take a *sharpened* form, a more committed and protagonist form, where the firm supports its client in an adversarial situation.

4.70   An auditor's client is in principle the company and its shareholders. But his duty to that particular client must be set in the context of the wider public interest which requires him (through Companies Act requirements and the Auditing Practices Board pronouncements) to provide an opinion as to whether a set of financial statements gives a true and fair view. That true and fair view must be an objective one, not tailored to or influenced by the needs of the client.

---

*Any application of paragraph 4.66 to actuarial valuations affecting pension schemes, funds and costs, including the application of Statement of Standard Accounting Practice, Accounting for Pension Costs (SSAP24), will not apply for the time being. The matters are being reviewed by the Chartered Accountants Joint Ethics Committee prior to issue of further guidance.

4.71   Hence advocacy in any sharpened form is likely to appear to the beholder to be incompatible with the particular objectivity required by the audit reporting role. And in fact, particular advocate roles, though adopted with objective judgement, may tend subsequently to form a degree of commitment in the professional's mind which may make it difficult to return to the objectivity required for reporting.

4.72   The following examples are provided to illustrate the classes of professional services or other activity which may give rise to these sharper forms of advocacy:

(a)   **The recommendation, or promotion, of shares** requires the adoption of a posture of advocacy in relation to the company concerned which cannot be compatible with objectivity in reporting. To recommend or promote shares usually requires a mental commitment to views or assertions about the strengths and qualities of the company. These views or assertions may have been reached by objective consideration, but once adopted the mental commitment does not readily permit a return to either the appearance or the reality of dispassionate and objective judgement.

(b)   **By extension, leading a corporate finance team which takes the responsibility for recommending or promoting shares** will be incompatible with objectivity in reporting. For this reason the Statement, Corporate Finance Advice (1.203), contains what amounts to a prohibition on the provision of such services to a company on which the firm reports.

(c)   **The adoption of an extreme position on any issue of accounting principles, taxation or other matter of professional judgement** will always raise the risk of putting the practitioner into a position of sharpened advocacy. This will be heightened if it becomes necessary for the firm to support the extreme position in adversarial proceedings such as litigation, Takeover Panel proceedings, or negotiations with government revenue departments. Such a position may both raise doubts in the minds of observers and make it genuinely difficult for a firm to preserve its own audit objectivity on the topics at issue.

4.73   The central issue for auditors in illustration (c) is the identification of what is or may become an extreme position.

Members should endeavour to foresee such difficulties arising, and either avoid the extreme position or suggest to the company that it may seek alternate advisers to perform any roles requiring adversarial advocacy. It should be re-emphasised that there is nothing inherently unethical in advocating an extreme position on a client's behalf, if it can be supported by objective evidence. But it may be improper to perform such advocacy while at the same time asserting that the objectivity of the audit role has been maintained. In some situations separation of roles between different partners may provide a degree of internal safeguards, but practitioners should recognise the risk of bringing themselves and the profession into disrepute by entering into a situation where a position of advocacy appears to indicate a position of commitment or a bias in state of mind which is not consistent with the objective state of mind required for a reporting role.

The threat of over-familiarity

4.74 Members are warned in particular of the dangers of being inadvertently drawn into the provision of management functions where a range of services has been provided to an audit client over a period of years. A member should be careful not to go beyond the advisory role and drift into the management sphere.

Involvement in management

4.75 The objections to an auditor becoming involved in a management role should be apparent. *All* of the threats to objectivity discussed above would affect the auditor who took management decisions, and their combined weight would make it virtually impossible for a member to claim to have retained objectivity in audit reporting.

4.76 A situation may arise where advice is tendered by the practitioner over a long period and the management of the company so frequently accepts and acts on the advice that it becomes difficult to separate the role of management from that of adviser. Members should ensure in every case that management accepts the judgements involved as its own after adequate consideration.

4.77 A practitioner would need to consider the position carefully if the firm were invited to design systems affecting operations on which the commercial success of the company depended. It might even be desirable for management to consider taking an expert second opinion if the advice from the auditor and the ensuing management judgements were crucial to the company's financial and operational success. Many practitioners would judge that objectivity could be preserved in the audit only if management was well qualified with its own expertise to make all the operating judgements involved in the adoption and implementation of the system and if there were, among other internal safeguards, a considerable degree of separation of the system designers from the audit team.

4.78 Recruitment of key financial and administrative staff for an audit client company is an instance where a firm should proceed with care. Whilst it is acceptable for the firm to advertise for and interview prospective staff and produce a 'short list' and recommendations, the final decision in every case as to whom to engage should be left to the client.

Area of risk – acting for a prolonged period of time

4.79 Where the same engagement partner acts for an audit client company for a prolonged period of time, a familiarity threat will arise.

Safeguards in relation to acting for prolonged period of time

4.80 Firms should, in relation to the audit of 'listed companies' as defined in paragraph 7.6, ensure that no audit engagement partner remains in charge of such an audit for a period exceeding seven consecutive years. An audit engagement partner (see paragraph 7.1) who has ceased under the above provision to act as such should not return to that role in relation to that audit until a minimum of five years has passed, but is not precluded from other involvement with the client.

4.81 A limited degree of flexibility over timing may be acceptable in circumstances where audit engagement partner continuity is especially important. Examples could include major changes to a company's structure or management, or its involvement in a takeover, which would otherwise coincide with the partner change.

4.82 Because rotation of the audit engagement partner cannot be implemented by a sole-practitioner auditor, or by small firms where there is only one 'responsible individual', these should, in relation to the audit of listed companies, be prepared to demonstrate that the following procedures have been carried out:

(a) internal review, at least annually, coupled with

(b) external consultation (see paragraph 3.7).

Companies and clients other than those specified in 4.80 (above)
4.83 The threat to a firm's objectivity arising from audit engagement partners continuing in such roles for a prolonged period remains in relation to all clients and not merely those specified in paragraph 4.80; the same considerations apply in respect of senior audit staff. Members should, therefore, establish adequate review machinery along the lines indicated in paragraphs 3.2 to 3.7 above, including an annual review, in order to satisfy themselves that each engagement may properly be accepted or continued.

5.0 Section B – Objectivity and independence in financial reporting and similar non-audit roles

5.1 There are roles other than the audit, in which a member is required to report with similar authority on financial matters, and to which, therefore, the considerations referred to in Section A (above) apply, as follows:

Financial reporting
5.2 The considerations which make it essential for a member's objectivity to be safeguarded when he or she carries out an audit are also relevant to other financial reporting assignments requiring a professional opinion, including reporting assignments where a document has been prepared in contemplation that a third party may rely on it.

5.3 For reports commissioned by management for management's internal use only, see paragraphs 6.1 to 6.3 below.

Litigation support
5.4 A member called upon to report or undertake work in connection with civil proceedings or with criminal prosecution should appreciate that such work may be tendered as evidence in a court of law and/or involve the member in giving evidence upon oath. The objectivity of such a member should, therefore, be safeguarded when he or she accepts and carries on such an assignment.

Specialist valuation
5.5 The objectivity of a member who carries out a specialist valuation, the results of which may be included in financial accounts or public documents, needs to be

safeguarded, and similar considerations apply to those set out in Section A in relation to the carrying out of an audit.

Arbitration

5.6   It is a requirement of law that an arbitrator must act independently of the parties and of the issues involved in an arbitration.

Due diligence

5.7   Guidance on the considerations involved in the provision of due diligence work is dealt with in Statement **1.203**, Corporate Finance Advice.

6.0   Section C – Objectivity and independence in professional roles other than those covered in Sections A and B

6.1   This section deals with work other than the work covered by Sections A and B of this Statement including:

●   taxation services;

●   preparation of accounts;

●   corporate advisory services other than the preparation of documents for public use;

●   management consultancy services; and

●   reporting to management/secondment to management.

6.2   Independence in the sense in which it is sometimes applied to audit assignments (Section A above) is not essential to the work referred to in the previous paragraph, provided that the practice is not also auditor to the client and objectivity is not impaired. Guidance on the considerations relating to possible conflicts of interest is given in Statement **1.204**, Conflicts of Interest.

6.3   There are nevertheless certain factors which by their nature are a threat to objectivity in any professional role. Accordingly the following considerations referred to in Section A (above) apply to the professional assignments referred to in paragraph 6.1 above:

Area of risk – family and other personal relationships

6.4   **An objective approach to any assignment may be subject to self-interest or familiarity threats as a consequence of a family or other close personal or business relationship.**

6.5   Objectivity in relation to any assignment may be subject to a self-interest threat where a mutual business interest exists with a client company or with an officer or employee of the company. The safeguards indicated in paragraphs 3.2 to 3.7 should be implemented as appropriate. In addition, adequate disclosure of any conflict of interest arising should be made to all relevant parties.

Area of risk – loans

6.6 **An objective approach to any assignment may be subject to a self-interest threat if a firm, or any principal of the firm should directly or indirectly make any loan to, or receive a loan from a client, or give or accept any guarantee in relation to a debt of the client, firm or principal.**

6.7 A firm or a principal of the firm should not receive any loan from a client. This is because the size of the perceived self-interest threat arising in such circumstances is generally seen as being too great to be offset by any available safeguards. Nor should a firm or principal make any loan to a client, although this restriction does not normally apply to any account in credit with a client clearing bank or similar financial institution.

6.8 The above advice is not intended to preclude a loan, overdraft or home mortgage being accepted from a client financial institution in the normal course of business and on normal commercial terms provided that, where the loan is applied so as to subscribe to partnership capital or where the loan is made to an engagement partner, the significance of the loan is not such as to cast doubt on the objectivity of the practice in performing the role or roles which it is contracted to discharge.

6.9 Similar considerations apply where there are significant overdue fees from a client or group of connected clients.

Area of risk – goods and services; hospitality or other benefits

6.10 **A self-interest threat arises where anyone in the firm receives goods or services, or hospitality from a client. These should not, therefore be accepted by a firm or by anyone closely connected with it unless the value of any benefit is modest.**

Beneficial interests in shares and other investments

6.11 **A self-interest threat to the objectivity of a member or firm will arise in relation to any investment in a company or undertaking with which the firm has a professional relationship, and the safeguards set out in paragraphs 3.2 to 3.7 above should be implemented as appropriate. Where the value of the investment is material to the financial circumstances of the investing member or firm, they should cease to advise professionally – see paragraph 3.9.**

Business advisers

6.12 **Where a member or a practice acts as business adviser to a client, he, or she, or it may invest in that client, and, if the client is a company, act as sponsor or promoter of its shares, provided that the relationship is clearly declared to relevant parties.**

Discussion

6.13 Members who hold office in a client company, or have a comparable business relationship with a client, should be aware of the dangers inherent in seeking to combine such a role with that of adviser, having regard to the self-interest threat to their objectivity. In such circumstances, members should be aware of the distinctive nature of each of the roles in which they are professionally engaged, and employ safeguards, including disclosure where appropriate (see paragraphs 3.2 to 3.7, and also Statement **1.204**, Conflicts of Interest).

7.0   Section D – Definitions

Audit engagement partner
7.1 An audit engagement partner is one who has the responsibility for the conduct of the audit and for the issue of an opinion on the financial statements. A member who has an equivalent responsibility in a corporate practice should be regarded on the same basis.

Closely connected
7.2 Paragraphs 4.23 and 4.50 (above) refer to a 'close connection' of a principal of a firm. This phrase has been chosen because it is not practicable in an advisory document such as this to stipulate precisely the relationships beyond which the independence of a practitioner may be put in jeopardy. Persons not related in any way by blood or marriage, for example, may nevertheless enjoy a friendship closer than many blood relationships. Conversely, two spouses may have lived apart from each other for many years without any financial dependency upon or contact with each other.

7.3 Bearing in mind, however, the need to maintain not merely independence, but also the manifest appearance of independence, the following persons will normally be regarded as closely connected with a person, namely:

(a) his or her spouse (other than a spouse from whom he is separated) or cohabitee or, in the case of a shareholding, other than a spouse or cohabitee of whose financial affairs he has been denied knowledge;

(b) his minor children, including stepchildren;

(c) a company in which he has a 20 per cent or more interest.

7.4 In the event of a complaint a member will be presumed to have knowledge of the financial affairs of his spouse or cohabitee unless he demonstrates the contrary.

7.5 The following persons will normally be regarded as being closely connected with a firm:

(a) a partner or, in the case of a corporate practice, a director or shareholder;

(b) a person closely connected with (a) above;

(c) an employee of the firm.

For the reasons mentioned earlier these categories are not exhaustive of the relationships which might threaten independence.

Listed companies
7.6 For the purposes of this Statement, reference to listed companies should be taken to include the following:

(a) companies whose shares or securities have been admitted to listing by a recognised stock exchange;

(b) companies whose equity share capital is marketed under the regulations of a recognised stock exchange, e.g. companies whose shares are dealt with on the Alternative Investment Market.

Other public-interest companies

7.7 Various paragraphs of this Statement refer to 'other public-interest companies'. Where this occurs the phrase is intended to include those unlisted companies and organisations, in both the private and public sectors, which are 'in the public eye' because of their size or product or service they provide. Examples of such companies and organisations would be large charitable organisations and trusts, major monopolies, duopolies, building societies, industrial and provident societies or credit unions, deposit-taking organisations, and those holding investment business client money.

Principal

7.8 References to a principal of a firm include the following:

(a) a partner;

(b) a sole practitioner;

(c) a director of a corporate practice, who deals directly or indirectly with accountancy clients or potential accountancy clients of the firm; and

(d) an employee of a corporate firm who is:

- a responsible individual within the meaning of the Audit Regulations;
- a licensed insolvency practitioner;
- defined as such in circumstances determined by Council.

Shares and shareholdings

7.9 Reference to shares and shareholdings should be taken to include debenture and other loan stock and the equivalent, and rights to acquire shares, debenture or other loan stock. Shareholdings also include options to purchase or sell such securities. A person's holdings include holdings by a nominee on behalf of that person or by a trust created by that person for his or her personal benefit. Shareholdings in parent, subsidiary or associated companies of a client company should normally be regarded on the same basis as shareholdings in the client company itself. However, if the firm is auditor only of a company or companies which taken together constitute an insignificant part of a group, independence of the parent company etc. is not required.

Specialist valuations

7.10 For the purposes of this Statement 'Specialist Valuations' include actuarial valuations, valuations of intellectual property and brands, other intangible assets, property and unquoted investments but, not:

i valuations under Section 108, Companies Act 1985 of the consideration to be received for the allotment by a public company of shares otherwise than in cash; or

ii   valuations under Section 109, Companies Act 1985, of the consideration to be received by a public company or any consideration other than cash to be given by the company, for the transfer during the initial period of a non-cash asset to the company or another.

The term 'specialist valuation' is not intended to cover the giving of normal advice or discussion, or work of a confirmatory nature, on the adequacy of provisions or the valuation of assets or liabilities which are to be determined by the directors or others.

1.202 Insolvency Practice

This Statement applies only to practising members, affiliates and, where appropriate, employees of practising members.

Introductory Note
1.0   The Fundamental Principles direct the attention of each member to the overriding importance in his or her professional life of integrity and objectivity. These elements are as important in the acceptance and conduct of insolvency work as in any other area of professional life. In certain insolvency roles the preservation of objectivity needs to be protected and demonstrated by the maintenance of a member's independence from influences which could affect his objectivity. Before a member accepts or carries out those roles, which are detailed in the guidance which follows, the member must not only be satisfied as to the actual objectivity which he can bring to his judgement and decisions, but must also be mindful of how his acceptance and conduct will be perceived by others.

1.1   In applying the following guidance, members should also have regard to the existing provisions of the Guide to Professional Ethics, in particular in relation to conflicts of interest (Statement 1.204) and obtaining professional work (Statement 1.211) to the extent that those matters have not been addressed in this Statement.

1.2   For the purpose of this Statement 'principal' means a sole practitioner, a partner in a firm or a director of a corporate practice.

Obtaining Insolvency Work
2.0   The offer or payment of commission to a member's employee or to another public accountant in return for the introduction of a client is generally permitted under Statement 1.211. However the special nature of insolvency appointments makes the payment or offer of any commission for, or the furnishing of any valuable consideration towards the introduction of insolvency appointments inappropriate.

2.1   The attention of members is also drawn to section 164 of the Insolvency Act 1986, which creates an offence punishable by a fine of offering to a member or creditor of a company any valuable consideration with a view to securing nomination as a liquidator, and to the Insolvency Rules 1986, which provide for remuneration to be disallowed to a liquidator (rule 4.150) or trustee (rule 6.148) whose appointment has been procured by improper solicitation.

Solicitation for proxies
3.0   In addition to any statutory consequences which it may incur, solicitation for insolvency work in any way amounting to that which a reasonable person would regard as harassment, or otherwise so as to represent a breach of the guidance of paragraphs 1.0, 3.0 and 4.0 of Statement 1.211 renders a member liable to reference to the Investigation Committee.

Professional independence and the acceptance of insolvency appointments
General
4.0   The following paragraphs refer to specific situations in which a member may not properly accept appointment. In situations other than those dealt with a member should only accept office in any insolvency role sequential to one in which the member or his practice or a current employee of the practice has previously acted after giving careful consideration to the implications of acceptance in all the circumstances of the case, and satisfying himself that objectivity is unlikely to be compromised, by a prospective conflict of interest or otherwise. If he remains in doubt as to his position the member should seek advice from CAASE via its Secretariat.

4.1   The attention of members is drawn to the statutory disqualification on acting as an insolvency practitioner in section 390 of the Insolvency Act 1986.

Joint appointments
4.2   A member who is invited to accept an insolvency appointment jointly with another practitioner should be guided by similar principles to those set out in relation to sole appointments. Where a member is specifically precluded by the guidance which follows from accepting an insolvency appointment as an individual, a joint appointment will not render the appointment acceptable.

Appointment as supervisor of a company voluntary arrangement, administrator, administrative or other receiver.
5.0   Where there has been a material professional relationship (as to which see paragraphs 8.0 to 8.3) with a company no principal or employee of the practice should accept appointment as supervisor of a voluntary arrangement, administrator or administrative or other receiver in relation to that company. (See also paragraphs 8.4 and 8.5, 20.0 and 20.1 (below).)

Appointment as supervisor of individual voluntary arrangement, trustee in bankruptcy or trustee under a Deed of Arrangement
6.0   Where there has been a material professional relationship (as to which see

paragraphs 8.0 to 8.3) with a client, no principal or employee of the practice should accept appointment as supervisor of a voluntary arrangement or as trustee in bankruptcy or as a trustee under a deed registered under the Deeds of Arrangement Act 1914 in relation to that client. (See also paragraphs 20.0 and 20.1 (below).)

Appointment as liquidator

7.0 Where there has been a material professional relationship (as to which see paragraphs 8.0 to 8.3) with a company, no principal or employee of the practice should accept appointment as liquidator of the company if the company is insolvent. Where the company is solvent such appointment should not be accepted without careful consideration being given to all the implications of acceptance in the particular case, and a member should satisfy himself that the directors' declaration of solvency is likely to be substantiated by events. (See also paragraphs 20.0 and 20.1 (below).)

Material professional relationship

8.0 A material professional relationship with a client, such as is referred to in paragraphs 5.0 to 7.0 (above) arises where a practice or, subject to the provisions of paragraphs 20.0 and 20.1 (below), a principal or employee of a practice, is carrying out, or has during the previous three years carried out, material professional work for that client. Material professional work would include the following:

(i) where a practice or person has carried out, or has been appointed to carry out, audit work for a company or individual to which the appointment is being considered; or

(ii) where a practice or person has carried out one or more assignments, whether of a continuing nature or not, of such overall significance or in such circumstances that a member's objectivity in carrying out a subsequent insolvency appointment could be or could reasonably be seen to be prejudiced.

8.1 A material professional relationship with a company or individual (as referred to in paragraphs 5.0 to 7.0) includes any material professional relationship with companies or entities controlled by that company or individual or under common control, where the relationship is material in the context of the company or individual to whom appointment is being sought or considered. A material professional relationship could also arise where a practice or person has carried out professional work for any director or shadow director of a company of such a nature that a member's objectivity in carrying out a subsequent insolvency appointment in relation to that company could be or could reasonably be seen to be prejudiced.

8.2 In forming views as to whether a material professional relationship exists, members should have regard to existing or previous relationships with firms with which they are, or have been associated which might affect or appear to affect their objectivity, including relationships whereby they or their firm are held out by name association or other public statements as being part of a national or international association.

8.3 A member should take reasonable steps prior to his acceptance of any insolvency appointment to ascertain whether any of the above work has been performed.

Appointment as investigating accountant at the instigation of a creditor

8.4   A material professional relationship would not normally arise where the relationship is one which springs from the appointment of the practice by, or at the instigation of, a creditor or other party having an actual or potential financial interest in a company or business to investigate, monitor or advise on its affairs provided that

(a)   there has not been a direct involvement by a principal or employee of the practice in the management of the company or business, and

(b)   the practice has its principal client relationship with the creditor or other party, rather than with the company or proprietor of the business, and the company or the proprietor of the business is aware of this.

8.5   If the circumstances of the initial appointment are such as to prevent the open discussion of the financial affairs of the company with the directors, an investigating member of the other principal in the practice may be called upon to justify the property of their acceptance of the subsequent appointment

Conversion of members' voluntary winding up into creditors' voluntary winding up

9.0   Where a member has accepted appointment as liquidator in a members' voluntary winding up and is obliged to summon a creditors' meeting under section 95 of the Insolvency Act 1986 because it appears that the company will be unable to pay its debts in full within the period stated in the directors' declaration of solvency, the member's continuance as liquidator will depend on whether he believes that the company will eventually be able to pay its debts in full or not.

(a)   If the company will not be able to pay its debts in full and the member has previously had a material professional relationship with the company such as is set out in paragraphs 8.0 to 8.3 above, he should not accept nomination under the creditors' winding up.

(b)   If the company will not be able to pay its debts in full but the member has had no such material professional relationship, he may accept nomination by the creditors and continue as liquidator with the creditors' approval, subject to giving the careful consideration as to the implications, etc. referred to in paragraph 4.0 (above).

(c)   If the member believes that the company will eventually be able to pay its debts in full he may accept nomination by the creditors and continue as liquidator. However if it should subsequently appear that this belief was mistaken the member must then offer his resignation, and may not accept re-appointment if he has previously had a material professional relationship with the company.

Insolvent liquidation following appointment as administrative or other receiver

10.0   Where a principal or employee of a practice (subject to the provisions of paragraphs 20.0 and 20.1 (below) is, or in the previous three years has been administrative receiver of a company, or a receiver, under the Law of Property Act 1925 or otherwise, of any of its assets, no principal or employee of the practice should accept appointment as liquidator of the company in an insolvent liquidation. This restriction does not apply where the previous appointment was made by the Court. However, before a Court-appointed receiver accepts subsequent appointment as liquidator, he should give careful consideration as to whether his objectivity could be open to question and, if so, the appointment should be refused.

Liquidation following appointment as supervisor of a voluntary arrangement or administrator

11.0 Where a member, or any principal or employee of his practice, has been supervisor of a voluntary arrangement or administrator of a company, the member may, if the considerations indicated in paragraph 4.0 (above) are satisfied, accept appointment as liquidator if so nominated by the creditors or appointed by the Secretary of State under Section 137 of the Insolvency Act 1986.

12.0 However where the relevant previous role is that of administrator, the member should not accept nomination or appointment as liquidator unless either:

(a) the member has the support of a creditors' committee appointed under section 26 of the Insolvency Act 1986, or

(b) he has the support of a meeting of creditors called either under the Act or informally, of which all known creditors have been given notice.

Bankruptcy following appointment as supervisor of individual voluntary arrangement

13.0 Where a member, or any principal or employee of his practice, has been supervisor of a voluntary arrangement in relation to a debtor, the member may, provided the considerations indicated in paragraph 4.0 (above) are satisfied, accept appointment as trustee in bankruptcy of that debtor provided that is effected by a general meeting of the creditors under the provisions of section 292(1)(a) of the Insolvency Act 1986 or if the member has been appointed by the Court under section 297(5) of the Act or by the Secretary of State under Section 296 of the Act.

Administration following appointment as administrative receiver, or LPA or other receiver

14.0 Where a principal or employee of a practice (subject to the provisions of paragraphs 20.0 and 20.1 (below) is, or in the previous three years has been, an administrative receiver of a company, or a receiver, under the Law of Property Act 1925 or otherwise, of any of its assets, no principal or employee of the practice should accept appointment as administrator of the company, unless the previous appointment was made by the Court.

Supervision of a voluntary arrangement following appointment as administrative receiver

15.0 Where a principal or employee of a practice (subject to the provisions of paragraphs 20.0 and 20.1 (below) is, or in the previous three years has been, an administrative receiver of a company, no principal or employee of the practice should accept appointment as supervisor of a voluntary arrangement in relation to that company.

Audit following appointment as supervisor of a voluntary arrangement, administrator or administrative or other receiver

16.0   Where a principal or employee of a practice (subject to the provisions of paragraphs 20.0 and 20.1 (below) has acted as supervisor of a voluntary arrangement, administrator or administrative receiver of a company or receiver of any of its assets, no principal or employee of the practice should accept appointment as auditor of the company for any accounting period during which the supervisor, administrator or receiver acted.

Pension Schemes of companies in liquidation, administration or receivership – appointment of 'Independent Trustee'

17.0   A member should not appoint a principal or employee of his practice, or any close connection of any of the above or of himself, as 'Independent Trustee' of the pension scheme of a company of which he is the liquidator, administrator or administrative or other receiver. A member should be aware of the threat to objectivity if he were to engage in regular or reciprocal arrangements in relation to such appointments with another practice or organisation.

Other potential conflicts of interest

(i)   Group, Associated and family-connected companies

18.0   Members should be particularly aware of the difficulties likely to arise from the existence of inter-company transactions or guarantees in group, associated or 'family-connected' company situations. Acceptance of an insolvency appointment in relation to more than one company in the group or association may raise issues of conflict of interest. Nevertheless it may be impracticable for a series of different insolvency practitioners to act. A member should not accept multiple appointments in such situations unless he is satisfied that he is able to take steps to minimise problems of conflict and that his overall integrity and objectivity are, and are seen to be, maintained.

(ii)   Relationships between insolvent individuals and insolvent companies.

19.0   A member who, or a principal or employee of whose practice, is acting as insolvency practitioner in relation to an individual may be asked to accept an insolvency appointment in relation to a company of which the debtor is a major shareholder or creditor or where the company is a creditor of the debtor. It is essential, if the member is to accept the new appointment, that he should be able to show that the steps indicated in paragraph 18.0 have been taken. Similar considerations apply if it is the company appointment which precedes the individual appointment.

Transfer of principals and employees including practice merger

20.0   When two or more practices merge, principals and employees of the merged practice become subject to common ethical constraints in relation to accepting new insolvency appointments to clients of either of the former practices. However existing appointments which are rendered in apparent breach of the guidance by such merger need not be determined automatically, provided that a considered review of the situation by the practice discloses no obvious and immediate conflict, such as a potential need to sue a new colleague.

20.1 Where a principal or an employee of a practice has, in any former practice, undertaken work upon the affairs of a company or debtor in a capacity which is incompatible with an insolvency assignment of his new practice, he should not personally work or be employed on that assignment, save in the case of an employee of such junior status that his duties in the former practice did not involve the exercise of any material professional judgement or discretion.

Personal relationships

21.0 The current legislation includes specific duties to report on the conduct of directors or shadow directors of an insolvent company. (See for example the requirement under section 7(a) of the Company Directors Disqualification Act 1986 to report 'unfit' conduct to the Secretary of State, and sections 213 and 214 of the Insolvency Act 1986 on fraudulent trading and wrongful trading). A member should have regard at all times to the spirit of the guidance on independence in Statement 1.201 and should not accept an insolvency appointment in relation to an individual or a company where any personal connection with the individual or with a director, former director or shadow director is such as to impair or reasonably appear to impair the member's objectivity. The attention of members is also drawn to the definitions relating to persons 'connected' with a company in sections 249 and 435 of the Insolvency Act 1986.

Relationship with a debenture holder

22.0 A member should, in general, decline to accept an insolvency appointment in relation to a company if he or a principal or employee of the practice has such a personal or close and distinct business connection with the debenture holder as might impair or appear to impair the member's objectivity. It is not considered likely that a 'close and distinct business connection' would normally exist between an Insolvency Practitioner and, for example, a clearing bank or major financial institution. However, such a close and distinct business connection would exist where a member, or a principal or employee of the practice holds an insolvency appointment in relation to such a bank or financial institution.

Purchase of the assets of an insolvent company or debtor

23.0 The Insolvency Rules 1986 contain prohibitions on members of a liquidation or creditors' committee acquiring any asset in the estate of an insolvent company or debtor (save with leave of the Court or the committee). Save in circumstances which clearly do not impair his objectivity, a member appointed to any insolvency appointment in relation to a company or debtor should not himself acquire directly or indirectly any of the assets of the company or debtor nor knowingly permit any principal or employee of his practice, or any close relative of the member or of a principal or employee, directly or indirectly to do so.

23.1 Where a contract is already in existence between the insolvent company or debtor and a principal or an employee of the member's practice, the member should seek guidance from the CAASE Secretariat as to the propriety of accepting the appointment.

1.203 Corporate Finance Advice

This Statement applies to all members. Council has approved this revised Statement, which is effective from 1 April 1995.

Its objective is to provide ethical guidance that will safeguard corporate finance clients by ensuring that they can rely on the objectivity and integrity of the advice given to them by members.

Introductory Note

1.0 Corporate finance activities are wide-ranging in their nature and members are frequently involved in giving corporate finance advice, to both audit and non-audit clients. The role and nature of advice expected of a member may change in character when the client becomes involved in or anticipates a particular transaction, such as a takeover bid or issue of securities. It is at that point that problems of independence and conflict of interest can arise. Members should be aware that, when acting as sponsor subject to 'the Listing Rules' (see paragraph 3 below), some corporate finance activities such as promoting, marketing or placing securities contain so strong an element of advocacy as to be incompatible with the objectivity required for the reporting roles of an auditor or reporting accountant*. Where the activities of an auditor or reporting accountant are restricted to ensuring clients' compliance with the Listing Rules there should be little threat to its objectivity. The guidance which follows is designed to assist members who find themselves advising in these and related circumstances.

1.1 Members giving corporate finance advice are required to comply with the requirements of the Financial Services Act 1986 and, where applicable, the Institute's Investment Business Regulations.

The Takeover Panel

2.0 Attention is drawn to the need to comply with the *City Code on Takeovers and Mergers* (the City Code) and the *Rules Governing Substantial Acquisitions of Shares* (the SARs), which are expressly applied to professional advisers as well as to those engaged in the securities market. Members' attention is particularly drawn to the annexed Guidance Note: *Compliance with the City Code on Takeovers and Mergers.*

---

*The Chartered Accountants' Joint Ethics Committee is consulting on whether (a) due diligence assignments should be added to the above reporting roles and (b) there may be a serious threat to a firm's objectivity if it should extend its role too deeply into management by leading the team of professionals whose functions include the roles of marketing or promoting the transaction. Co-ordination tasks, such as initiating and organising meetings, issuing timetables and reporting progress, seem unlikely to threaten reporting objectivity. But the role of a project manager who took on responsibility for the success or failure of the issue or sale might pose a more serious threat.

The Stock Exchange

3.0 Members' attention is drawn to the London Stock Exchange's 'The Listing Rules' (Yellow Book) in particular when acting as a sponsor.

Objectivity and Integrity

3.0A Provided that a member maintains objectivity and integrity throughout, both in regard to the client and to other interested parties, there can be no objection to his or her accepting an engagement which is designed primarily with a view to advancing the client's case.

Conflicts of Interest

4.0 It may be in the best interests of a client company for corporate finance advice to be provided by its auditor and there is nothing improper in the auditor supporting a client in this way. There are however a variety of situations in which conflict can arise.

4.1 It would not on the face of it be improper for the firm to continue to act as auditor to both parties in a takeover situation, even if the takeover were contested.

City Code Transactions

4.2 A firm may find itself acting as auditor or corporate finance adviser for two or more parties involved in a takeover subject to the City Code. For the firm to cease to act for a client within the limited period of the takeover, on the basis that conflict might arise, could damage the client's interests.

Accordingly in such circumstances a firm may continue to act for more than one party as auditor, as reporting accountants on any profit forecast, and in the provision of incidental advice consistent with these roles. However the firm should not act as lead adviser for any party involved or issue a critique of a client's accounts, and should implement proper safeguards (see paragraph 6.0 below).

4.3 For the purposes of the preceding paragraph the 'lead adviser' is the firm or person primarily responsible for advising on, organising and presenting an offer or the response to an offer. This definition would include the 'independent financial adviser' required by a defending company under Rule 3 of the City Code.

4.4 The attention of firms is also directed to those sections of the City Code dealing with conflict of interest, including the possession of 'material confidential information'. Members in doubt as to their position under the City Code should consult the Takeover Panel.

Transactions not Subject to the City Code

4.5 Where a takeover is not subject to the City Code, and there is no substantial public interest involved, a firm may, subject to the implementation of appropriate safeguards (see paragraph 6.0 below), continue to advise both sides. However the firm should ensure that the interests of minority shareholders are protected, and in such cases should consider the desirability of one company having a wholly independent adviser.

Promoting an Issue or Sale

4.6 A firm should not underwrite or promote an issue or sale to the public of shares or securities of a company on which it has reported or is to report. Neither should the firm undertake to accept nomination as auditor or reporting accountant of the company whose shares it is underwriting or promoting to the public. Involvement of this kind would endanger the independence of the firm in the audit and/or reporting function.

4.7 It is not inappropriate however:

(a) for an auditor or reporting accountant otherwise to assist a client in raising capital;

(b) for a firm to conduct an acquisition search, which could identify another client as a target, provided the search is based solely on information which is not confidential to that client;

(c) for an auditor or reporting accountant to fulfil the responsibilities of a sponsor as set out in Chapter 2 of the Yellow Book providing this does not include underwriting or promoting, including pricing, of the issue or sale of shares or securities to the public; or

(d) for an auditor or reporting accountant otherwise to provide independent advice, to a client or its professional advisers in connection with the issue or sale of shares or securities to the public.

Avoiding Conflicts of Interest

5.0 All reasonable steps should be taken to ascertain whether a conflict of interest exists or is likely to arise in the future between a firm and its clients, both in regard to new engagements and to the changing circumstances of existing clients, and including any implications arising from the possession of confidential information. Relationships with clients and former clients need to be reviewed before accepting a new appointment and regularly thereafter. A relationship which ended over two years before is unlikely to constitute a conflict. Where it is clear that a material conflict of interest exists a firm should decline to act as corporate finance adviser.

5.1 It would be neither reasonable nor necessary to discontinue acting in any capacity in anticipation of every potential conflict. It could in some instances give rise to harmful rumour or speculation for a firm to disengage from a situation before a bid had become public knowledge.

5.2 Where there appears to be a conflict of interests between clients but after careful consideration the firm considers that the conflict is not material and unlikely seriously to prejudice the interests of any of those clients, the firm may accept or continue the engagement, but not without first informing the clients concerned. Unless security considerations dictate otherwise it would be prudent for this to be in writing.

5.3 A firm should not act or continue as lead adviser for two or more clients if the disclosure called for in the previous sub paragraph would seriously prejudice the interests of a client.

5.4 Where a conflict of interests is likely seriously to prejudice the interests of a client an engagement should not be accepted or continued even at the informed request of the clients concerned.

5.5 Where a firm is required for any reason to disengage from an existing client it should do so as speedily as practicable having regard to the interests of the client.

Safeguards

6.0 Where a firm acts or continues to act for two or more clients following disclosure in accordance with the previous paragraphs, all reasonable steps should be taken to manage the conflict which arises and thereby avoid any adverse consequences. These steps should include the following safeguards except to the extent that they are inappropriate:

(a)   the use of different partners and teams for different engagements;

(b)   all necessary steps to prevent the leakage of confidential information between different teams and sections within the firm;

(c)   regular review of the situation by a senior partner or compliance officer not personally involved with either client; and

(d)   advising the clients to seek additional independent advice.

6.1 Any decision on the part of a sole practitioner should take account of the fact that the safeguards at (a) to (c) of the previous paragraph will not be available to him or her. Similar considerations apply to a small practice.

Sponsors

6.2 When a firm accepts the responsibilities of a sponsor set out in Chapter 2 of the Yellow Book in respect of a client where it acts as auditor or reporting accountant, it should adopt steps described in paragraph 6.0 above and additionally set up procedures to review and to identify any potential conflicts of interest which could compromise the firm's objectivity.

Documents for Client and Public Use

7.0 Where in the course of corporate finance advice a firm prepares information for a client – for example a critique of the accounts of another company – it may be called upon to do so:

(a)   in a document which is for the consumption of the client only;

(b)   in order to assist the client to produce a document which will go out solely under the client's name and authority, whether including quotations from the original document or not; or

(c)   as part of a document which is to be published over the name of the member firm.

7.1   Any statements or observations in a document prepared for a client must be such as, taken individually and as a whole, are justifiable on an objective examination of the available facts.

7.2   In the case of a document prepared solely for the client and its professional advisers, it should be a condition of the engagement that the document should not be disclosed to any third party without the firm's express permission.

7.3   Any document whether for private or public use should be prepared in accordance with normal professional standards of integrity and objectivity and with a proper degree of care.

7.4   A firm is, in the absence of any indication to the contrary, entitled to assume that the published accounts of the company on which it is commenting have been prepared properly and in accordance with all relevant Accounting standards. Where scope for alternative accounting treatment exists, and the accuracy of the comment or observation is dependent on an assumption as to the actual accounting treatment chosen, that assumption must be stated, together with any other assumptions material to the commentary. Where the firm is not in possession of sufficient information to warrant a clear opinion this should be declared in the document.

7.5   A firm must take responsibility for anything published under its name, and the published document should make clear the client for whom the firm is acting. To prevent misleading or out-of-context quotations, it should be a condition of the engagement that, if anything less than the full document is to be published, the text and its context should be expressly agreed with the firm.

7.6   A firm should ensure that public documents and circulars include prominently the name of the brokers, investment bank or other advisers responsible for promoting or underwriting the share or securities described in the document or circular, where different from that firm which has accepted the roles of sponsor, in order to make abundantly clear the roles undertaken by the various advisers.

Fees

8.0   Where a member undertakes an engagement for a fee which is contingent upon the successful outcome of a transaction such as a bid, offer, purchase, sale or raising finance, he or she should take particular care to ensure that the arrangements do not prejudice his or her independence and objectivity with regard to any other role which he or she may have, notably as auditor or reporting accountant of either the bidder or the target. (Members are referred to 1.210, *Fees*.)

Overseas Transactions
9.0   This Statement has been drafted with regard to the situation in the United Kingdom and the Republic of Ireland. Members should apply the spirit of the guidance, subject to local legislation and regulation, to overseas transactions of a similar nature.

Members in Business

10.0 1.220, *The Ethical Responsibilities of Members in Business*, includes (at paragraphs 2.0 and 2.1) the following Guidance:

Objectivity
The concept of independence, which is central to the role of the practising accountant, has no direct relevance to the employed member. (Even for the practising accountant independence is not an end in itself: it is essentially a means of securing a more important end, namely an objective approach to work). The requirement for objectivity, however, is of equal application to all members. **Without the capacity of being fully independent of his employer it is all the more important that the employed member should strive constantly to maintain objectivity in every aspect of his work.**

Objectivity is described in Fundamental Principle 2 as the state of mind which has regard to all considerations relevant to the task in hand but no other. It follows that the interests of a member's employer should no more affect the objectivity of a member's judgement in a professional matter than his own interests.

Observance of this guidance is particularly necessary in the context of corporate finance activities, especially when making public statements and commenting on takeover situations.

Annex to 1.203

Guidance Note

Compliance with the City Code on Takeovers and Mergers
(See paragraph 2.0 of 1.203)

1.0 A member who provides takeover services for clients is required to comply with the *City Code on Takeovers and Mergers* ('the City Code'), and *Rules Governing Substantial Acquisitions of Shares* ('the SARs'), and with all rulings made and guidance issued under them by the Panel on Takeovers and Mergers ('the Panel').

1.1 Accordingly a member proposing to provide takeover services to a client should at the outset:

(a) explain that these responsibilities will apply; and

(b) include in the terms of the engagement recognition of the member's obligation to comply with the City Code and the SARs including any steps which the member may be obliged to take in performing those responsibilities. A specimen clause for the engagement letter is set out in paragraph 4.0 below.

1.2 As regards contractual relationships existing at the date of publication of this Guidance Note, members should seek to amend the relevant engagement letter to include such wording. Where this does not prove possible, members should inform clients of their intention to comply with the City Code and the SARs. If the client objects to this, the member should carefully consider the reasons given for such objection and then consider whether it is appropriate to continue to act for the client. In such a situation it may be necessary for the member to take separate legal advice.

Scope of Takeover Services

2.0 In this Guidance, 'takeover services' means any professional services provided by a member to a client in connection with a transaction to which the City Code or the SARs applies.

2.1 In the case of accountants, the kinds of activities most commonly relevant for this purpose include:

(a) acting as financial adviser to one of the parties (for example, as 'Rule 3 adviser' to the offeree company);

(b) reporting on profit forecasts and/or valuations for the purposes of takeover documents;

(c) approving investment advertisements issued in connection with a takeover transaction for the purposes of s.57, Financial Services Act 1986;

(d) conducting acquisition searches for clients, and introducing clients to other parties with a view to potential acquisitions;

(e) advising in relation to acquisitions and disposals of securities to which the City Code may apply.

2.2 Whilst the City Code does not define precisely the range of activities and transactions within its scope, paragraph 4 of the Introduction to the City Code describes the companies and transactions which are subject to the City Code. In practice, those engaging in providing takeover services rarely experience difficulty in determining whether the City Code is or may be relevant to the activities proposed to be undertaken for any particular client.

Special Responsibilities

3.0 A member who has provided or is providing takeover services to a client should:

(a) supply to the Panel any information, books, documents or other records concerning the relevant transaction or arrangement which the Panel may properly require and which are in the possession or under the control of the member; and

(b) otherwise render all such assistance as the member is reasonably able to give to the Panel,

provided that in each case the relevant information, books, documents or other records were acquired by the member in the course of the member providing the relevant takeover services.

3.1 Except with the consent of the Panel, a member should not provide or continue to provide takeover services for any person if the Panel has stated that it considers that the facilities of the securities markets in the United Kingdom should be withheld from that person and has not subsequently indicated a change in this view. A person to whom this paragraph applies will normally have been named in a statement published by the Panel, *inter alia*, for the purposes of Rule 5-48 (i) of the *Conduct of*

Business Rules of The Securities and Futures Authority.

3.2 If members have included in the engagement letter agreed with their client a provision to the effect of that recommended in paragraph 1.1(b) above, they will be able to discharge their responsibilities under paragraphs 3.0 and/or 3.1 above, without any breach of confidentiality or duty to the client. While members should include such a provision, it is recognised that, on occasion, compliance with such responsibilities may still involve a breach of confidentiality to a third party or a breach of some other duty owed to the client. In such circumstances this Guidance Note is not applicable.

Specimen Clause for Engagement Letters

4.0 *The Client agrees and acknowledges that where the services provided by the Firm relate to a transaction within the scope of the City Code on Takeovers and Mergers ('the City Code'), or the Rules Governing Substantial Acquisitions of Shares ('the SARs'), the Client and the Firm will comply with the provisions of the Code and the SARs and will observe the terms of the Guidance Note published by the Institutes of Chartered Accountants relevant to such services or transactions. In particular, the Client acknowledges that:*

(a) *if the Client or its advisers or agents fail to comply with the City Code or the SARs then the Firm may withdraw from acting for the client; and*

(b) *the Firm is obliged to supply to the Panel any information, books, documents or other records concerning the services or transaction which the Panel may properly require.*

The Financial Services Act 1986

5.0 The provision of corporate finance services will usually require authorisation under the Financial Services Act 1986. However, this guidance note applies to all members and firms, whether authorised or not.

1.204 Conflicts of Interest

This Statement applies only to practising members, affiliates and where appropriate, employees of practising firms.

Introductory Note

1.0 This Statement deals with two types of conflict of interest: conflicts between the interests of a firm and a client and conflicts between the interests of different clients. (Members' attention is drawn to 1.203, *Corporate Finance Advice*.)

The implications arising from the possession and use of confidential information are separate issues: members are referred to 1.205, *Confidentiality*.

Conflict Between a Firm's Interests and those of its Client

2.0 **A firm should not accept or continue an engagement in which there is or is likely to be a significant conflict of interests between the firm and its client.**

Discussion

2.1 Whether a significant conflict of interest exists will depend on all the circumstances of the case. The test is whether a reasonable observer, seized with all the facts, would consider the interest as likely to affect the objectivity of the firm. However, any material financial gain which accrues or is likely to accrue to the firm as a result of the engagement (otherwise than in the form of fees or other reward from the client for its services, or commission, etc, properly earned and declared under the terms of paragraph 3.0 below), will always amount to a significant conflict of interests for the purpose of paragraph 2.0 above.

Commission

3.0 **A member should not allow his or her judgment to be swayed by the fact that he will receive a commission, fee, reward or other benefit from a third party by advising a client to pursue one course rather than another.**

3.1 **Where a member becomes aware that any commission, fee or reward, may be earned by the firm or anyone in it or by an associated firm for the introduction of a client, or as a result of advice given to a client, the client should be informed in writing:**

(a)   **that commission is likely to result and, when the fact is known, that such commission, fee or reward will be received, and**

(b   **as early as possible, of its amount and terms.**

3.2 Members are reminded that where a fiduciary relationship under common law exists at the time between a member and a client, the member is legally bound to account to the client for any commission, fee, reward or other benefit received. The Institute is advised that the effect is that a member will require the informed consent of the client if the member is to retain the commission, fee or reward, etc, or any part of it. If members are in doubt as to whether the circumstances give rise to a fiduciary relationship, they are recommended to take appropriate legal advice.

(More information as to the legal considerations involved is given in 1.314.)

(For the special case of Investment Business Advice, see the relevant section of the Investment Business Regulations).

Other Benefits

4.0 **A client should be informed in writing as soon as practicable of any benefit other than commission, fee or reward received or to be received, by the firm or anyone in it, or by any associate of the firm, in return for the introduction of a client or as a result of advice given to a client.**

Discussion

4.1 A client should be made aware whenever a member is acting otherwise than as an independent adviser. In such a case the client should be told of any relevant relationship with an associate of the firm, and the extent to which the member's services or advice are constrained thereby. If a firm, for example, recommends to a client a computer organisation or FIMBRA member which is an associate of the firm: (a) the client should be made aware of the connection; and (b) the firm should take special care that the advice given to the client to use the associate is in the client's best interests.

Conflict Between Interests of Different Clients

5.0 There is, on the face of it, nothing improper in a firm having two or more clients whose interests may be in conflict. In such a case however, the work of the firm should be so managed as to avoid the interests of one client adversely affecting those of another. Where the acceptance or continuance of an engagement would, even with safeguards, materially prejudice the interests of any client the appointment should not be accepted or continued, or one of the appointments discontinued.

Discussion: Identification of Conflict Between Clients' Interests

5.1 All reasonable steps should be taken to ascertain whether any conflict of interests exists or is likely to arise in the future, both in regard to new engagements and to the changing circumstances of existing clients. Relationships with existing clients need to be considered before accepting a new appointment and regularly thereafter. The nature of the engagements is relevant in this connection. (Members are referred to 1.203, *Corporate Finance Advice*.)

Disclosure

5.2 Wherever there is identified a significant conflict between the interests of different clients or potential clients sufficient disclosure should be made to the clients or potential clients concerned together with details of the safeguards proposed under paragraph 5.3 below so that they may make an informed decision as to whether to engage the firm or continue their relationship with the firm. Where adequate disclosure is not possible by reason of the constraints of confidentiality the firm should not accept or continue both assignments.

Safeguards

5.3 Where a firm becomes aware of a possible conflict between the interests of two or more clients all reasonable steps should be taken to manage it and thereby avoid any adverse consequences. These steps should include the following safeguards except where they are inappropriate:

(a)   the use of different partners and teams of staff for different engagements;

(b)   standing instructions and all other steps necessary to prevent the leakage of confidential information between different teams and sections within the firm;

(c)   regular review of the situation by a senior partner or compliance officer not personally involved with either client; and

(d)   advising at least one or all clients to seek additional independent advice.

Sole Practitioners and Small Firms

5.4   Any decision on the part of a sole practitioner should take account of the fact that the safeguards at (a) to (c) of the previous paragraph will not be available to him or her. Similar considerations apply to a small firm.

Disengagement

5.5   Wherever a firm is required by paragraphs 2.0 or 5.2 above to disengage from an existing engagement it should do so as speedily as is compatible with the interests of the clients concerned.

1.205   Confidentiality

This Statement applies to all members.

Improper Disclosure

1.0   Information confidential to a client or employer acquired in the course of professional work should not be disclosed except where consent has been obtained from the client, employer or other proper source, or where there is a legal right or duty to disclose.

Discussion

1.1   Questions which may arise as to the propriety of disclosing clients' affairs are dealt with at length in 1.306. Paragraphs 7-25 of that section set out the general legal position in relation to disclosure of information acquired in the course of a professional assignment. Similar guidance for members in business regarding disclosure of an employer's affairs is set out in 1.402, in particular paragraphs 3-18. Disclosure so far as it concerns an auditor is dealt with in Auditing Guideline 418.

1.2   Where a member is in doubt as to whether he or she has a right or duty to disclose he should, if appropriate, initially discuss the matter fully within his firm or organisation. If that is not appropriate, or if it fails to resolve the problem, he should consider taking legal advice and/or consult the Institute via the director of CAASE or IMACE as appropriate.

Improper Use of Information

2.0 A member acquiring or receiving confidential information in the course of his

or her professional work should neither use nor appear to use that information for his personal advantage or for the advantage of a third party.

Discussion

2.1 When a member changes his or her firm or employment he is entitled to use experience gained in the previous firm or employment but not confidential information acquired there.

2.2 A member should not deal in the shares of a company with which he has a professional association at such a time or in such a manner as might make it seem that he was turning to his own advantage information obtained by him in his professional capacity.

2.3 It may be a criminal offence in certain circumstances to use confidential information for an improper purpose. See, for example, the Company Securities (Insider Dealing) Act 1985.

1.206   Changes in a Professional Appointment

This Statement applies only to practising members, affiliates and, where appropriate, employees of practising firms. (It replaces Guidance previously contained in the Guide to Professional Ethics and Guidance for Members in Practice and is effective from 1 January 1995).

Recurring Work

1.0   Clients have the right to choose their auditors and other professional advisers, and to change to others if they so desire. Nevertheless it is necessary, in the interests of both the public and the existing auditor or adviser* and prospective auditor or adviser, for a member who is asked to act by a prospective client in respect of an audit or recurring reporting assignment, or the provision of recurring accounting services and taxation work of a compliance nature, to communicate with the existing auditor or adviser, and for the latter to reply promptly as to any considerations which might affect the prospective auditor or adviser's decision whether or not to accept appointment.

1.1   Members should undertake the same procedures with non-member appointees as they would with members.

1.2   Members invited to undertake work additional to that carried out by another professional adviser should consult paragraphs 4.0 to 4.2 (below).

---

*Where there is no existing auditor or adviser the procedures apply equally to the previous auditor or adviser.

Discussion

Communication – The procedure of 'professional enquiry'

1.3   The purpose of finding out the background to the proposed change is to enable the member to determine whether, in all the circumstances, it would be proper for him or her to accept the assignment. In particular, members nominated as auditors will wish to ensure that they do not unwittingly become the means by which any unsatisfactory practices of the company or any impropriety in the conduct of its affairs may be enabled to continue or may be concealed from shareholders or other legitimately interested persons. Communication is meant to ensure that all relevant facts are known to the member who, having considered them, is then entitled to accept the nomination if he wishes so to do. The need to communicate exists whether or not the existing auditor or adviser intends to make representations to the proprietors, including his statutory right to make representations to the shareholders, and whether or not he or she still continues to act. Communication of the facts to a prospective auditor or adviser cannot relieve the existing auditor or adviser of his duty to continue to press on the client his views on any technical or ethical matters which may have led him into dispute with the client, nor does it affect the freedom of the client to exercise his right to a change of auditor or adviser.

1.4   When a member is first approached by a prospective client he should explain that he has a professional duty, if asked to act or be nominated, to communicate with the existing auditor or adviser.

1.5   When nominated or asked to act the member should ask the client to inform the existing auditor or adviser of the proposed change and, at the same time, to give the latter written authority to discuss the client's affairs with the member.

1.6   The member should then write to the existing auditor or adviser, seeking information which could influence his decision as to whether or not he may properly accept appointment. The existing auditor or adviser has no responsibility for that decision, and there is no 'professional clearance' which he can give or withhold.

1.7   If the client fails or refuses to grant the existing auditor or adviser permission to discuss the client's affairs with the proposed successor the existing auditor or adviser should report that fact to the prospective auditor or adviser who should not accept nomination/appointment.

1.8   The existing auditor or adviser should answer without delay the communication from the prospective auditor or adviser. If there are no matters of which the latter should be aware, the existing auditor or adviser should write to say that this is the case. If, however, there are such matters (see paragraph 1.15 below) he should inform the prospective successor of those factors within his knowledge of which, in his opinion, the latter should be aware. It is not sufficient to state that unspecified factors exist. The existing auditor or adviser might prefer to explain these factors orally and the prospective auditor or adviser should be prepared to confer with the existing auditor or adviser if the latter so desires, and each should make their own record of such a discussion.

1.9   If an issue of conflicting viewpoints between the client and himself or herself has been raised by the existing auditor or adviser in his reply, the prospective successor should discuss the conflict with the client and satisfy himself either that the client's view is one which he can accept as reasonable, or that the client will accept that the member might have to express a contrary opinion.

1.10 Where the existing auditor or adviser does not respond within a reasonable time the prospective successor should endeavour to contact the existing auditor or adviser by some other means, for instance by telephone or by facsimile. Should this fail, and where the prospective successor has no reason to believe there are untoward circumstances surrounding the change, he should send a final letter by recorded delivery service stating that unless he receives a reply within a specified time he will assume that there are no matters of which the existing auditor or adviser is aware that should be brought to his attention. A member who accepts nomination in such circumstances is not precluded from complaining to the Institute that the existing auditor or adviser did not respond to his enquiry letter.

1.11 If the prospective auditor or adviser is satisfied that he can properly act, and is prepared to accept nomination/appointment, he should so inform the client.

1.12 Where the member decides to accept nomination/appointment having been given notice of any matters which are the subject of contention between the existing auditor or adviser and the client he should be prepared, if requested to do so, to demonstrate to the Investigation Committee that proper consideration has been given by him to those matters.

1.13 Members' attention is drawn to Statement of Auditing Standards: *Fraud and error* (SAS 110).

Statutory Provisions
1.14 Firms must adhere to the statutory provisions relating to any change in an audit appointment, in particular those contained in the Companies Act 1985, Sections 391 to 394, and, for the Republic of Ireland, the Companies Act 1963, Sections 160,161 and Companies Act 1990, Sections 183-186 and for Northern Ireland: the Companies Northern Ireland Order 1986, Articles 399-401(B) and in particular the proposed auditor should ensure that the previous auditor has validly vacated office.

Communication
1.15 The matters referred to in paragraph 1.8 above would, where relevant, include the following, that

(a) reasons for the change advanced by the client of which the existing auditor or adviser is aware are not in accordance with the facts (as understood by the latter);

(b) the proposal to displace the existing auditor or adviser arises in his opinion because he has carried out his duties in the face of opposition or evasion/s in which important differences of principle or practice had arisen with the client;

(c) the client, its directors, or employees may have been guilty of some unlawful act or default, or that any aspect of their conduct which is relevant to the carrying out of an audit or assignment ought, in the opinion of the existing auditor or adviser, to be investigated further by the appropriate authority (see Statement 1.306 regarding unlawful acts or defaults by clients);

(d)   the existing auditor or adviser has unconfirmed suspicions that the client or its directors or employees have defrauded the Inland Revenue, Customs & Excise or others (see paragraph 1.19 regarding privilege and Statement 1.306 regarding unlawful acts or defaults by clients);

(e)   the existing auditor or adviser has serious doubts regarding the integrity of the directors and/or senior managers of the client company;

(f)   the client, its directors, or employees have deliberately withheld information required by the existing auditor or adviser for the performance of his duties or have limited or attempted to limit the scope of his work;

(g)   the existing auditor proposes to bring to the attention of members or creditors circumstances surrounding the proposed change of auditor.

1.16   The incumbent should not refuse to communicate, or delay his reply, on the grounds that:

(a)   a prospective auditor has obtained nomination in contravention of this guidance; or

(b)   the incumbent auditor or adviser has a genuine belief, whether justified or not, of having been unfairly treated by the client.

Further Points

'Unacceptable reasons'

Unpaid fees
1.17   The existence of unpaid fees is not of itself a reason why a prospective auditor or adviser should not accept nomination/appointment. If he does accept, it may be appropriate for him to assist in any way open to him towards achieving a settlement of outstanding fees; whether or not he does so is entirely a matter for his own judgement in the light of all the circumstances.

Confidentiality
1.18   The prospective auditor or adviser should ordinarily treat in confidence any information provided by the existing auditor or adviser. However, it may be essential to the fulfilment of a prospective auditor's or adviser's obligations that he should disclose such information. It may, for example, be unavoidable for the prospective auditor or adviser to disclose to officers or to employees of the client matters brought to his attention by the predecessor firm which need to be properly investigated. Such disclosure should be no wider than is necessary.

Defamation
1.19   Council has advised that an existing auditor or adviser who communicates to a

prospective successor matters damaging to the client or to any individuals concerned with the client's business will have a strong measure of protection were any action for defamation to be brought against him, in that the communication will be protected by qualified privilege. This means that he should not be liable to pay damages for defamatory statements even if they turn out to be untrue, provided that they are made without malice. The chances of an incumbent being held to have acted maliciously are remote provided that:

(i)   he states only what he sincerely believes to be true; and

(ii)   he does not make reckless imputations against a client or individuals connected with it which he can have no reason for believing to be true.

Joint Auditor
1.20   A member whose firm is nominated as a joint auditor should communicate with all existing auditors and be guided by similar principles to those set out in relation to nomination as an auditor. Where it is proposed that a joint audit appointment becomes a sole appointment, the surviving auditor should communicate formally with the other joint auditor as though for a new appointment.

Vacancy
1.21   A member whose firm is invited to accept nomination on the death of a sole practitioner auditor should endeavour to obtain such information as he may need from the latter's alternate (where appropriate), the administrators of the estate or other source.

Transfer of Books and Papers

2.0   A replaced auditor or adviser should transfer promptly to the client, or to his successor after the latter has been duly appointed, all books and papers which are in his possession and which belong to the client unless he is exercising a lien thereon for unpaid fees. Members should be aware that the courts have held that no lien can exist over books or documents of a registered company which, either by statute or by articles of association of the company, have to be available for public inspection (see Statement 1.302 paragraphs 18 et seq). Members attention is drawn to Statement 1.210, Fees, in particular paragraph 3.2.

Co-operation with a Successor

3.0   The incoming auditor or adviser often needs to ask his predecessor for information as to the client's affairs, lack of which might prejudice the client's interests. Such information should be promptly given and unless there is good reason to the contrary, such as a significant amount of work involved, no charge should be made.

Additional Work

4.0   A member invited to undertake recurring or non-recurring work which is additional to and related to continuing work carried out by another professional

adviser should notify that other professional adviser of the work he has been asked to undertake.

Discussion

4.1 It is generally in the interest of the client that the existing auditor or adviser be aware of the nature of the additional work being undertaken. The existing adviser will be provided with the opportunity to communicate with the member to provide information, lack of which might otherwise prevent the additional work from being carried out effectively. Additionally, such notification could affect the way an existing auditor or adviser discharges his continuing responsibilities to his client.

4.2 Notification should always be given unless the client advances reasons which persuade the firm that, in all the circumstances, the existing adviser should not be informed.

4.3 Provision of an opinion on the application of accounting standards or principles is dealt within Statement 1.213, Second and Other Opinions.

1.207 Consultancy

This Statement applies only to practising members, affiliates and, where appropriate, employees of practising firms.

1.0 If a member in practice (the practitioner) obtains the advice of a member (the consultant) on a consultancy basis on behalf of a client, the consultant or any practising firm with which he or his consultancy organisation is associated should not, without the consent of the practitioner, accept from that client within three years of completion of the consultancy assignment, any work which was, at the time the consultant was first retained in relation to that client's affairs, being carried out by the practitioner.

2.0 The same considerations apply where a practitioner introduces one of his clients to the consultant for the purposes of consultancy.

1.208 Agencies

This Statement applies only to practising members, affiliates and, where appropriate, employees of practising firms.

Introductory Note

1.0   The guidance which follows is intended to assist members in their arrangements with building societies and others, whether or not these arrangements fall within the operation of the Financial Services Act 1986. Members who are in doubt as to their ethical position are encouraged to seek advice of their Institute. Members in authorised firms, i.e. authorised by one of the Institutes of Chartered Accountants, are reminded that the Institute's Investment Business Regulations (the 'Regulations') impose restrictions on the persons who may be appointed as an appointed representative (within the meaning of section 44 of the Act) or an authorised firm.

Appointed Representatives: Unauthorised Firms

2.0   Practising members who are not authorised to conduct investment business, whilst not covered by the Regulations, should not accept appointment as an appointed representative of another person authorised to conduct investment business under the Act.

Building Society Agencies

3.0   The acceptance by a member or member firm of an agency may present a threat to professional independence.

Particular problems are attendant upon agencies within building societies because building societies are expanding the range of services they offer to the public beyond a deposit and similar business, to include providing services related to insurance and unit trust investments which are themselves subject to the Financial Services Act. References to 'building societies' in the following paragraphs include references to other deposit taking organisations.

3.1   Before accepting or continuing an agency with a building society members should satisfy themselves:

(a)   that their professional independence would not be compromised; and

(b)   that such acceptance or continuance would not be rendered inappropriate by the nature of the services they are to provide under the agency, or the manner in which those services may be brought to the attention of the public.

Considerations for Firms
4.0   Even though advice on building society deposits falls outside the Financial Services Act, members advising generally on the disposition of clients' funds require a breadth of investment expertise and the freedom to advise which can only be offered by an independent intermediary, authorised under the Act.

4.1   Though a firm's operation of a building society agency, restricted to simple forms of deposit taking, does not require authorisation under the Financial Services Act, the mere presence of agency signs and literature, together with the public perception arising from publicity of the increasing range of building society products and services, could produce a real danger that the firm might be perceived, by the public, as holding itself out as carrying on investment business. Should an unauthorised firm actually stray into the provision of investment business advice as defined by the Act, it could be committing a criminal offence.

4.2 For these reasons it will, in normal circumstances, be inappropriate for an unauthorised firm to continue or to enter into any form of agency or other arrangement with a building society. However, if an unauthorised firm believes that its own special circumstances justify such an agency or arrangement, it will need to be able to demonstrate, in the event of complaint, that it has implemented safeguards and procedures adequate to guard against any breach of the law or any threat to its independence.

Other Problem Areas

5.0 Where a firm has an arrangement with a building society that arrangement should relate solely to deposit taking. It should not, for example, relate to the products of a particular insurance company or unit trust organisation for which the building society is an appointed representative.

5.1 Problems can occur even in the case of an agency limited to deposit taking, if it appears to be a vehicle whereby the services of only one insurance company or unit trust organisation are provided or publicised. Firms should, therefore, take steps to avoid such an impression being given and such steps should include ensuring that any display of literature contains an appropriate range of competitive products. A firm should be aware at all times of the need to advise in the clients' best interest. This is particularly important where a firm is considering recommending the associated products of a building society with which it has an agency.

5.2 In the interests of professional independence firms should not, in any circumstances, conduct their practices from premises which give the appearance of being a building society office.

5.3 Firms should not be a party to an exclusive agency by which they are constrained or induced to funnel all funds received by them for investment into a single building society.

Mortgage Borrowing: 'Clients' Best Interests'
6.0 A member may be asked by a client to advise on the comparative benefits of mortgage borrowing from a number of building societies, the repayment arrangements for which may be associated with endowment or other insurance schemes offered by the society on an appointed representative basis. In considering the mortgage offer of a particular building society, the member should look at the overall attributes of the 'package' offered. Special care is needed to ensure the objectivity of his or her advice when a member who holds an agency with a building society, which is itself the appointed representative of a life office, is considering recommending a 'package' offered by that building society.

Members' Own Arrangements with Building Societies

7.0 Members should not enter into any financial arrangements with a building society either personally or through their firm which would prejudice the independence of themselves or their firm.

7.1 Members should not accept appointment as agents of a building society of which their firm is auditor. (See 1.201, *Integrity, Objectivity and Independence*).

Commission
8.0 The attention of members is drawn to paragraphs 3.1-3.2 of 1.204, *Conflicts of Interest*.

Directorship of a Building Society

9.0 Members are warned of the possible threat to independence which may occur when a practising member accepts appointment as a director of a building society which is not authorised as an independent intermediary under the Financial Services Act.

Other Agencies
10.0 Firms who enter into other agency agreements for the supply of services and products, such as for the supply of computer hardware or software, should bear in mind the advice in paragraph 3.1 (above) as to professional independence and paragraphs 3.1-3.2 of 1.204, *Conflicts of Interest.*

1.209   Associations With Non-Members

This Statement applies only to practising members, affiliates and, where appropriate, employees of practising firms.

Mixed Accountancy Practices

1.0 A member engaged in public practice with a non-member partner or fellow director of a company is responsible for ensuring that the non-member conforms to the ethical standards governing the provision by members of public accountancy services.

Use of Offices, Name etc

2.0 A member should so conduct his or her firm that a client or potential client cannot mistake it for any other firm or business and cannot mistake any other associated firm or business for his.

Discussion

2.1 In particular, a member should not allow a non-member conducting a separate firm or business to use the same office or telephone number as his own without the distinction between the two firms or between the firm and the business being made abundantly clear. Attention is drawn in this connection to the terms of 1.208, *Agencies*.

2.2 A member should not allow a non-member in carrying out professional work for which the member or his firm is not responsible the use of his firm's name or of his qualification or designatory letters and should take all reasonable steps to ensure that no such abuse takes place or is continued.

Work for, or Obtained through Non-Members

3.0 **A member should not enter into arrangements to provide public accountancy services to clients of another firm or to clients introduced by another firm of public accountants not controlled by chartered accountants ('the requesting firm') unless he or she has satisfied himself or herself that the requesting firm's professional work is obtained in accordance with ethical standards governing the provision by members of public accountancy services.**

Discussion

3.1 A member has a responsibility to ascertain that work referred in this manner is in accordance with ethical standards because a member must not do, or be seen to do, through others what he may not do himself. To this end a member should:

(a) personally make professional enquiries to satisfy himself that the work has not been initially procured in an unprofessional manner;

(b) satisfy himself as to the competence and professional standards of staff whose work it would be his duty to review;

(c) act and be seen to act independently where this is called for by 1.201, *Integrity, Objectivity and Independence*; and should

(d) ensure his right of direct access to the client and, in appropriate circumstances, render his own fee account to the client.

3.2 Where an invitation to conduct a statutory audit comes other than directly from the client, the firm should first ensure that it has been properly appointed in accordance with statute. It should be made clear to all interested parties on all relevant documents that the member/firm is acting as principal, with all that that function implies. In those circumstances, the member should deal directly with the client and should render his own fee account in addition to complying with the other requirements of paragraph 3.1 above.

1.210 Fees

Effective: 1 February 1994
This Statement applies only to practising members, affiliates and, where appropriate, employees of practising firms.

Introductory Note

1.0 The Institute has been advised that a member is entitled in law to charge for his or her services:

(i) such specific fee as he or she has agreed with the client; or

(ii) a fee calculated in accordance with any agreement with the client; or,

(iii) in the absence of an agreement, a fee calculated by reference to the custom of the profession.

1.1 In the last event it is customary, where the basis of the fee has not been agreed with a client, that a member should charge a fee which is fair and reasonable having regard to:

(a) the seniority and professional expertise of the persons necessarily engaged on the work;

(b) the time expended by each;

(c) the degree of risk and responsibility which the work entails;

(d) the priority and importance of the work to the client together with any expenses properly incurred.

1.2 The Institute does not set charge-out rates for its members or otherwise prescribe the basis for calculating fees, nor does it ordinarily investigate complaints relating solely to the quantum of fees charged. (For the special situation of investment business fees see Investment Business Regulations, in particular Regulation 2.36.) However, members have certain professional responsibilities in relation to fees as set out in the following paragraphs.

Fee Quotations and Estimates

2.0 A member should inform a client in writing prior to commencement of any engagement of the basis upon which any fee he proposes to charge that client for his services will be calculated and, on request and where practicable, the level of fees likely to be charged for any assignment.

Discussion
2.1 The member should, at the earliest opportunity, discuss and explain the basis on which fees will be calculated and, where practicable, the estimated initial fee. The arrangements agreed should be confirmed in writing, normally in an engagement letter,

including a confirmation of any estimate, quotation or other indication, and where the basis of future fees will differ from that of initial fees, the basis on which such fees will be rendered. Where there is no engagement letter the member should confirm the initial discussion in writing to the client as soon as practicable.

2.2 Fee proposals should be made only after proper consideration of the nature of the client's business, the complexity of its operation and the work to be performed.

2.3 The fact that a member has quoted a fee lower than another is not improper provided care is taken to ensure that the client has a full and complete understanding of:

(a) the services to be covered by the fee, and

(b) the basis on which the fee is to be determined both for the current and future years.

Audit Work

2.4 Firms obtaining work having quoted levels of fees which they have reason to believe are significantly lower than those charged by an existing auditor or quoted by other tendering firms, should be aware that their objectivity may appear to be threatened. Such firms should ensure that their work complies with Auditing Standards and Guidelines and Audit Regulations and, in particular, quality control procedures (SAS 240: Quality control for audit work). In the event of a complaint being made to the Institute (which might have arisen as a result of a Joint Monitoring Unit inspection), where fees were a feature in obtaining or retaining the work, firms should be prepared to demonstrate to the Investigation Committee that:

(a) the work done was in accordance with Auditing Standards; and

(b) the client was not misled as to the basis on which fees for the current year and subsequent years were to be determined.

Fee Information and Disputes

3.0 A member should furnish, either in the fee account or subsequently on request, and without further charge, such details as are reasonable to enable the client to understand the basis on which the fee account has been prepared.

3.1 Where fees rendered exceed, without prior agreement, a quotation or estimate or indication of fees given by a member by more than a reasonable amount, the member should be prepared to provide the client with a full and detailed explanation of the excess and to take steps to resolve speedily any dispute which arises.

3.2 A member whose fees have not been paid may be entitled to retain certain books and papers of a client upon which he has been working by exercising a lien and may refuse to pass on information to the client or his successor accountant until those fees are paid. However, a member who so acts should be prepared to take reasonable steps to resolve any dispute relating to the amount of that fee. In respect of any fee dispute members should be aware of the fee arbitration services offered by the Institute.

Percentage and Contingency Fees

4.0   Fees should not be charged on a percentage, contingency, or similar basis in respect of audit work, reporting assignments and similar non-audit roles incorporating professional opinions including expert witness assignments. Even for other work such methods of charging may be perceived as a threat to objectivity and should, therefore, only be adopted after careful consideration.

Discussion

4.1   In bankruptcies, liquidations, receiverships, administrations, voluntary arrangements and similar work the remuneration may, by statute or tradition, be based on a percentage of realisations or a percentage of distribution. Consequently, it may not be possible to negotiate a fee in advance or base it on the principle in paragraph 4.0 above.

4.2   In some circumstances, such as advising on a management buy-out, the raising of venture capital, acquisition search or sales mandates, fees cannot realistically be charged save on a contingency basis: to require otherwise would, in certain cases, deprive potential clients of professional assistance, for example where the capacity of the client to pay is dependent upon the success or failure of the venture.

4.3   Where work is subject to a fee on a contingency, percentage or similar basis the capacity in which a member has worked and the basis of his remuneration should be made clear in any document prepared by the member in contemplation that a third party may rely on it.

Investment Business

5.0   Fees for investment business services provided by authorised firms are also subject to the Investment Business Regulations.

Advertisements

6.0   The attention of members is drawn to the guidance contained in 1.211, Obtaining Professional Work, relative to the mention of fees in advertisements.

1.211   Obtaining Professional Work

This Statement applies only to practising members, affiliates and, where appropriate, employees of practising firms.

Practice Promotion

1.0   Subject to the guidance which follows a member may seek publicity for his or

her services, achievements and products and may advertise his services, achievements and products in any way consistent with the dignity of the profession in that he should not project an image inconsistent with that of a professional person trained to high ethical and technical standards.

Discussion: Advertising

1.1   Advertisements must comply with the law and should conform as appropriate with the requirements of the British Code of Advertising Practice, and the ITC and Radio Authority Code of Advertising Standards and Practice, notably as to legality, decency, clarity, honesty and truthfulness.

1.2   An advertisement should be clearly distinguishable as such.

1.3 The preceding considerations are of equal application to letterheads, invoices and similar practice documents.

Discussion: Fees

1.4   If reference is made in promotional material to fees, the basis on which fees are calculated, or to hourly or other charging rates, the greatest care should be taken to ensure that such reference does not mislead as to the precise range of services and time commitment that the reference is intended to cover. Members should not make comparisons in such material between their fees and the fees of other accounting practices, whether members or not.

1.5   The danger of giving a misleading impression is particularly pronounced when constraints of space limit the amount of information which can be given. For this reason it will seldom be appropriate to include information about fees in short advertisements.

1.6   A member may offer a free consultation at which levels of fees will be discussed.

Disparaging Statements

2.0   Promotional material may contain any factual statement the truth of which a member is able to justify but should not make disparaging references to or disparaging comparisons with the services of others.

Discussion

2.1   Particular care is needed in claims of size or quality. For example, it is impossible to know whether a claim to be 'the largest firm' in an area is a reference to the number of partners or staff, the number of offices or the amount of fee income. A claim to be 'the best' firm is subjective and unsubstantiable.

Harassment

3.0   A member should, under no circumstances, promote or seek to promote his or her services, or the services of another member, in such a way or to such an extent as to amount to harassment of a prospective client.

Cold Calling

4.0   In relation to audit or other financial reporting work* a member should not make an unsolicited personal visit or telephone call to a person who is not a client with a view to obtaining professional work from the non-client. Members seeking to obtain insolvency work should refer to the Insolvency Rules 1986 and 1.202, Insolvency Practice, in particular paragraphs 2.0 to 3.0.

Discussion

4.1   Promotional or technical material may be sent to non-clients by mail or other means, subject to paragraph 4.3 below. Such a distribution should not, in the case of audit or other financial reporting work, be followed by a personal visit or telephone call save at the specific request of the recipient.

4.2   The same constraints apply to direct mail as to other promotional or technical material. (See paragraphs 1.1–2.1 above.)

4.3   Unsolicited promotional or technical material should not be sent to a non-client by facsimile transmission or other electronic means.

4.4   A member may send a letter introducing his or her firm and its range of services to another professional adviser, such as a solicitor or banker, and follow it up by a telephone call or visit. Such a follow-up should not be made in respect of audit or other financial reporting needs of the professional adviser.

Introductions

5.0   A member should not give or offer any commission, fee or reward to a third party, not being either his or her employee or another public accountant governed by ethical standards comparable to those observed by members or in the context of investment business another authorised firm, in return for the introduction of a client. (For the special situation of introducing insolvency business, see 1.202, Insolvency, paragraphs 2.0-2.1.)

Responsibility for Promotional Activities

6.0   For the purpose of this Statement, promotional activities carried out in the name of a firm should be construed as promotional activities carried out by the individual principals of that practice, whether carried out personally or through agents.

Promotion of Investment Business

7.0   Obtaining investment business, including investment business corporate finance work, is governed by the Investment Business Regulations, in particular Regulations 2.42 to 2.46, 2.80 to 2.84 and Schedule 2.

---

*For definition of 'other financial reporting work' see paragraph 23.0, 1.201.

1.212 The Names and Letterheads of Practising Firms

This Statement applies only to practising members, affiliates and, where appropriate, employees of practising firms.

For the purpose of this Statement the term '**firm**' includes a partnership, a corporation and a sole practitioner, the main business of which is the provision of services customarily provided by chartered accountants and the term '**letterhead**' means any part of the firm's notepaper and documents used by the firm for communicating with clients or other parties.

1.0   Subject to the Bye-laws and the following guidance, a member may practise under whatever name or title he or she sees fit.

1.2   A practice name should be consistent with the dignity of the profession in the sense that it should not project an image inconsistent with that of a professional practice bound to high ethical and technical standards.

1.3   A practice name should not be misleading.

Discussion

1.4   It would be misleading for a firm with a very few offices to describe itself as 'international' merely on the ground that one of them was overseas. Similarly it would be misleading for a sole practitioner to add the suffix 'and Associates' to the name of his or her practice unless formal arrangements were agreed with two or more consultants or firms.

1.5   A practice name would be misleading if in all the circumstances there was a real risk that it could be confused with the name of another firm, even if the member(s) of the practice could lay justifiable claim to the name.

1.6   It has been the custom of the profession for members to practise under a firm's name based on the names of past or present members of the firm itself or of a firm with which it has merged or amalgamated. A practice name so derived will usually be in conformity with this guidance.

1.7   There is no objection to membership of a trading group being indicated on the firm's notepaper or elsewhere in proximity to the practice name. However, the name of such a firm should be clearly distinguishable from the name of an associated firm or group. Thus, it would be misleading for a member of a trading group to bear the same name as the group, but there could be no objection to a firm practising under its own name 'as a member of (a named) accountancy group'.

Use of the Description 'Chartered Accountants'

2.0   Use of the description 'Chartered Accountants' is governed by Bye-law 55 and the regulations made thereunder.

2.1   The description 'Chartered Accountants' should not form part of the name of a firm.

2.2 Firms entitled under Bye-law 44 and the Regulations to use the description 'Chartered Accountants' are encouraged to do so, on their letterheading, in advertisements and generally. A firm which describes itself as 'Chartered Accountants' on its note paper may include a list of the services it particularly wishes to offer. However it should not incorporate any of that list of services into the general description of the firm (e.g., 'Chartered Accountants and Tax Advisers') lest this should suggest that these services are not offered by other chartered accountants. [NOTE: claims to authority to work in reserved areas such as audit and investment business are governed by the appropriate regulations and in the case of insolvency work by the relevant legislation].

2.3 Principals in a firm describing itself as 'Chartered Accountants' should adopt a distinguishing name for any separate firm of public accountants in which they may practise which is not itself entitled to the description 'Chartered Accountants'.

Discussion: Legal Requirements
3.0 A practice letterhead must comply with partnership and company law as appropriate, and with the Business Names Act 1985.

Discussion: Overseas Firms
4.0 Overseas firms are required to comply with any local laws as to practice names so far as overseas offices are concerned. Subject thereto, they may describe themselves in any manner conformable to the practice of the profession locally provided that the principles set out in paragraphs 1.0 to 1.3 above are observed.

Discussion: New and Changed Names
5.0 Save where the name of a firm is based on the names of past or present members of the firm itself or of a firm with which it has merged or amalgamated, when a new firm is to be set up and when it is desired to change the name of an existing firm members are recommended, as a means of ensuring compliance with this guidance, to consult the Institute, as to the propriety of the proposed name.

Persons Named on Letterheads

6.0 It should be clear from the letterhead of a practice whether any person named thereon, other than persons named only in the name of the firm, is a partner of the practice, a sole practitioner or, in the case of a corporate practice, a director.

6.1 Firms should distinguish chartered accountants mentioned on the letterhead of a practice from persons not entitled to be so described by the use of designatory letters or otherwise.

6.2 No person named on the letterhead of a practice should be described by a title, description or designatory letters to which he or she is not entitled.

Authorised Firms
7.0 The attention of members of authorised firms is drawn to the provisions of the Institute's Investment Business Regulations and the Guidance Notes, in particular those relating to affiliates.

1.213   Second and Other Opinions

This Statement applies to all members

Specific Circumstances

1.0   Where the opinion of a member, whether in practice or otherwise, is sought on the application of accounting standards or principles to specific circumstances or transactions, either completed or contemplated, of an entity with which the member does not have an ongoing professional relationship to provide audit services, he should be alert to the possibility of his opinion creating undue pressure on the judgement and objectivity of the auditor. Accordingly he should seek to minimise the risk of giving inappropriate guidance by ensuring that he has access to all relevant information.

Discussion

1.1   When the opinion of a member is sought on an accounting treatment by or on behalf of a company or entity which is not an existing audit client, there is a danger that the opinion he expresses may not be based on the same set of facts as is available to the auditor, or may be based on inadequate evidence and that the opinion may be difficult to modify if further facts come to light. It is important, therefore, that the member whose opinion is sought in such cases should ascertain the circumstances of his being consulted and all the other available facts relevant to formulating a professional judgement. For this purpose he should contact the auditor to provide an opportunity for the latter to bring to his attention any relevant facts and should be prepared, given his client's permission, to provide a copy of his opinion to the auditor. If the company or entity seeking the opinion will not permit the member to communicate with the auditor then he should decline to act.

1.2   Not at issue are opinions provided pursuant to litigation, expert testimony and assistance provided to other firms and their clients jointly.

General Circumstances

2.0   A member giving an opinion on the application of accounting standards or principles, relating to a hypothetical situation and not based on the specific facts or circumstances of a particular organisation, should ensure that the nature of the opinion is made clear.

1.220   The Ethical Responsibilities of Members in Business

This Statement applies only to Members in Business.

References in this Statement to an '**employed member**' include reference to members, whether employed or not, who are engaged in work relevant to their qualification as a member otherwise than in a practising office.

1.0   An employed member owes certain legal duties towards his or her employer. Additionally, he or she has ethical duties towards his Institute and, in particular, he should observe the same *Fundamental Principles* and the same standards of behaviour and competence as apply to all other members of the Institute.

Discussion

1.1   The Introduction to the Guide to Professional Ethics and 1.205, *Confidentiality*, are also of application to the member in business and should be read in conjunction with this Statement.

1.2   All members, whether in business or not, are liable to disciplinary action under the Bye-laws.

Objectivity

2.0   The concept of independence, which is central to the role of the auditor, has no direct relevance to the employed member. (Even for the practising accountant independence is not an end in itself: it is essentially a means of securing a more important end, namely an objective approach to work.) The requirement for objectivity, however, is of equal application to all members. Without the capacity of being fully independent of his employer it is all the more important that the employed member should strive constantly to maintain objectivity in every aspect of his work.

2.1   Objectivity is described in Fundamental Principle 2 as the state of mind which has regard to all considerations relevant to the task in hand but no other. It follows that the interests of a member's employer should no more affect the objectivity of a member's judgement in a professional matter than his own interests.

Illustration

2.2   Any report for which an employed member is responsible (whether it bears his or her signature or not) should be prepared with integrity and objectivity. This means for example that, while a report prepared by an employed member may properly present only one side of the case (for example his employer's) and may present that case to its best advantage, the report should be accurate, truthful and, within its scope, both complete and balanced. It should not rely on ambiguities or half truths, but should be objectively justifiable and should not be based on unreasonable assumptions. (See also 1.203, *Corporate Finance Advice*.)

2.3   While an employed member must observe the terms of his employment, these cannot require him to be implicated in any dishonest transaction. If he is instructed or encouraged to engage in any activity which is unlawful he is entitled and required to decline.

2.4   In practice, there may be many 'grey areas', for example as to whether an activity is indeed unlawful and how best to deal with the situation. Advice on these matters is to be found in 1.402, *Professional Conduct in Relation to Defaults or Unlawful Acts by or on behalf of a Member's Employer.*

Financial and Other Involvement

3.0   An employed member should recognise the problems which may be created by financial involvements or personal relationships which, whether sanctioned by his or her contract of employment or not, could nevertheless by reason of their nature or degree threaten his objectivity. Where any doubt exists the involvement or relationship should be disclosed to the employer.

Discussion: Share Dealings
3.1   In owning and dealing in shares in any organisation in which he or she is employed or holds office an employed member is bound by certain statutes including the Company Securities (Insider Dealing) Act 1985. In addition he should take care to observe:

(a)   the requirements of The Securities and Futures Authority, the Panel on Takeovers and Mergers and similar regulatory bodies as appropriate; and

(b)   his own terms of service.

Illustration: Receiving Gifts
3.2   An employed member should be aware of the difficulties which may arise from the offer or the acceptance of any gift, favour or hospitality which may be intended to influence the recipient or which could be interpreted by a reasonable person in full possession of the facts as likely to have that effect. Subject to this, gifts, favours and hospitality of modest value may be accepted to the extent that they may be permitted by the member's employer.

Professional and Technical Standards

4.0   Fundamental Principle 4 calls for a member to carry out his or her professional work with proper regard for the technical and professional standards expected of him as a member. The standards referred to in Fundamental Principle 4 include Accounting Standards, the *City Code on Takeovers and Mergers* and the *Rules Governing Substantial Acquisition of Shares* and, where appropriate, the Rules and Regulations of The Securities and Futures Authority. However, an employed member who, in the performance of his professional work, may be subject to directions from his employers, may be faced with a conflict of loyalties in seeking to apply this Fundamental Principle. The difficulty is of particular importance where the outcome of the work is to be published.

4.1 When a member has sole responsibility for the preparation and approval of information, including management information, which is to be made public or is to become available, on however restricted a basis, outside the organisation to which it refers, he or she should ensure that such information complies with the standards referred to in Fundamental Principle 4 or, if it does not so comply, that the reasons for non-compliance are stated truthfully, unambiguously and fairly.

4.2 When his is not the sole responsibility, the employed member should use his best endeavours to achieve compliance or, if the information does not comply with the standards referred to in Fundamental Principle 4, to ensure that the reasons for non-compliance are stated truthfully, unambiguously and fairly.

Status
5.0 While the considerations set out above apply to all employed members, the more senior the position occupied by the member the greater will be his or her opportunity to influence events, practices and attitudes and thus the more onerous will be his responsibilities.

Advice
6.0 An employed member faced with any ethical problem may call upon his or her Institute for confidential advice.*

6.1 Members can subscribe to a legal fees insurance scheme which can in certain circumstances, underwrite their legal costs arising from litigation or anticipated litigation.**

---

*IMACE has a team of Advisers, all with relevant experience, drawn from the area of each District Society. IMACE aims to put members in touch with an Adviser within two working days of receipt of the request for help.

In addition to professional advice the IMACE service includes the provision, where necessary, of free legal advice to members. The Institute has appointed a panel of solicitors in large towns who will provide up to two and a half hours advice free to the industrial member who needs it in respect of his conduct or likely conduct in seeking to maintain professional standards. If the problem remains unresolved after the legal consultation the member and the appointed solicitor will be able to decide whether further legal advice is needed. The Institute's involvement with the solicitor ends at this point. Where matters arise which require legal advice other than on the maintenance of professional standards, the Institute can provide members with the names of recommended firms of solicitors.

A member wishing to consult IMACE should get in touch with the Director, IMACE, at 399 Silbury Boulevard, Central Milton Keynes, MK9 2HL.

**A member wishing to obtain such insurance cover should contact Accountancy Business Group, 40 Bernard Street, London WC1N 1LD. Tel. 0171 833 3291.

INDEX